*Writers' & Art*

# How to Hook

ABOUT THE AUTHOR

**James Rennoldson** has managed writersandartists.co.uk for seven years and
run dozens of 'How to Hook an Agent' events within this time, putting small
groups of writers in a room with some of the UK's leading literary agents to
discuss the manuscript submission process. Originally from Bridlington,
East Yorkshire, James has worked in publishing for close to a decade and
lives in south-east London with his wife and son.

*Writers' & Artists' Guide to*

# How to Hook
# an Agent

## Q&A HELP AND ADVICE FOR AUTHORS

James Rennoldson

BLOOMSBURY YEARBOOKS
LONDON · OXFORD · NEW YORK · NEW DELHI · SYDNEY

BLOOMSBURY YEARBOOKS
Bloomsbury Publishing Plc
50 Bedford Square, London, WC1B 3DP, UK

BLOOMSBURY, BLOOMSBURY YEARBOOKS, WRITERS' & ARTISTS' and
the Diana logo are trademarks of Bloomsbury Publishing Plc

First published in Great Britain 2020

A catalogue record for this book is available from the British Library

ISBN: PB: 978-1-4729-7007-7; eBook: 978-1-4729-7006-0

2 4 6 8 10 9 7 5 3 1

Typeset by Deanta Global Publishing Services, Chennai, India
Printed and bound in Great Britain by CPI (Group) UK Ltd, Croydon CR0 4YY

To find out more about our authors and books, visit www.bloomsbury.com
and sign up for our newsletters.

# CONTENTS

# Introduction

Every writer and every book has a different path, and this will always be the way. Consider all the variables at play: a book's subject matter; a writers' search for *that* narrative voice; finding a concept that will strike a chord with an intended audience; the personal circumstances and sensibilities of an author. This is not to say that writers who have produced at least a first draft, or a well-crafted non-fiction proposal, undergo entirely unique experiences. In fact, most writers find they tend to share three things in common. Firstly, there's 'the spark': the idea that lights the touchpaper and from which a manuscript begins to flow. Second, there's a compulsion to commit countless hours to producing a strong narrative. And last, the writer arrives at the precise moment at which this guide begins, the point when they start to think: *this is good. Someone might want to publish it. But how do I get it in front of them?*

In picking up this guide, chances are you're a writer who's been through all of the thought process above. Have you begun taking note of the publisher logos emblazoned on the spines of books similar to your own when you've been in a bookstore or library? Has your confidence – and belief – in the manuscript (or book proposal) gone from strength to strength as it's developed? Have you started to discuss the prospect of trying to get published with select friends or family? Perhaps you've clicked around publisher websites to try and find the direct phone number or email address of an editor to approach about your book? If you're an author of fiction or popular narrative non-fiction, you may have read versions of the following statement: *We do not accept unsolicited manuscript submissions. Writers must be represented by a literary agent to be considered by our editorial department.*

And so, the next stage of your manuscript's journey is revealed: you need to be represented by a literary agent. But what is a literary agent? Who do they work for? Do you have to pay them? Why is it so hard to get published? What will an agent do for me and my book anyway? How do I hook an agent?

*

In 2013, Writers & Artists held its first 'How to Hook An Agent' lunch – a half-day event in which four UK literary agents were asked to deliver two short seminars to unpublished writers, providing insight into the role they play for authors and to offer advice on the process of submitting a manuscript. Appetite for the event was huge, leading to the hosting of dozens more in the years that have followed.

Inspired directly by the straightforward and frank conversations that have become commonplace at these intimate events, *How to Hook an Agent* deliberately takes the form of an introductory and practical Q&A guide, and brings together over 180 questions asked by writers in the throes of chasing their publishing dream, amalgamating responses from the leading UK literary agents invited to offer their expertise. Moving beyond a simple step-by-step approach, this book offers everything you need to know about the role of the agent, how to identify which agents to approach and provides practical examples of how to put together an excellent submission package.

Furthermore, and with a nod to the candid nature of the advice on offer at our events, this guide also addresses the difficulties writers can face when seeking an agent; the typical financial breakdowns to expect from signing a representation agreement (and from any subsequent deal with a publisher); and next-step guidance for writers who have had their manuscript rejected.

In such a highly competitive and subjective industry, success can in no way be guaranteed. Gaining agent representation may not come your way directly as a result of reading this book. What this book *can* guarantee, by virtue of years of unique insight into this crucial stage in the publishing process, is that you have the information and perspective required to take the manuscript submission process in your stride and that you give your writing the chance of success it deserves.

# PART I

## *The role of the literary agent*

# What are literary agents and what do they do?

For writers trying to get published, the very concept of a literary agent can initially be a cause of frustration. You believe in your completed manuscript (or knockout book proposal) and work on the assumption that the next stage is to make contact with someone working at a publisher to see if they're interested in publishing it … only to find out you've assumed wrong. In fact, if you're writing fiction or non-fiction for the general book-buying marketplace, there's more to be done before your book lands in front of a commissioning editor.

It's at this point of your personal publishing story that you're directed towards literary agents: an intermediary group of people you don't know much about, all working for separate companies, each with different literary wants and needs, and many with slight variations in the way they'd like your work sent to them. After writing an *entire* book (no mean feat, published or not), it's understandable this unexpected extra step is one that might irritate. What's a literary agent? Who are they? How can I find one? Am I just being fobbed off because publishing is a closed shop? Is there a way to circumvent this whole thing and send my work to publishers direct?

But rather than railing against the process and succumbing to the negativity of writers who've had their work out on submission to agents for a long time, the best use of your time is to accept the integral role literary agents play within the publishing ecosystem and start finding out how you can become one of their clients. Agents are key players within the game you're entering, and almost certainly the best way for you to go if you are to become the author of a book bought and published in the traditional sense (which is to say the rights to your manuscript are acquired by a publisher, who then apply their editorial, design, production, distribution, marketing and publicity resources to turn it into a printed item of interest to your target market). This is because the role of the agent is one that ultimately benefits both writer and publisher. Writers represented by an agent see their manuscript improve and cross the desk of editors who have a good chance of being interested in it; they will receive invaluable guidance throughout their career; and, crucially, have peace of mind where rights, royalties and all contractual matters are concerned in negotiating with a publisher (given all agents have a vested interest in securing the best terms possible for books they take to the market on behalf of their authors, as they get a cut). Basically, what's best for the career and future earnings of a writer becomes what's best for an agent, too.

Publishers, meanwhile, directly benefit from the role of the literary agent in two ways. First, their editorial departments have been relieved of sifting through the 'slush pile', a dated industry term sometimes used to refer to unsolicited submissions. And second, publishing house editors can open manuscripts sent to them by agents with a degree of confidence in both the standard of writing, and that they're about to read a book in-keeping with the sort of title they're responsible for publishing.

It's thus easy to see why agents are integral to the process of new fiction and commercial non-fiction finding its way to publishers. In effect, they are 'matchmakers' that get the best possible deal and the best editor for authors, and they bring new talent the way of publishers.

Yet occupying that pivotal position doesn't come easy. Most agents are inundated with unsolicited submissions and, by sheer necessity, are extremely selective of the writers they choose to represent. This book uses a conservative estimate of an agent receiving around fifty unsolicited manuscript submissions each week. If you imagine reading these submissions alongside office admin, networking events and all that comes with the management of an existing list of published authors, it's all too obvious that an agent's time is at a premium. And to amplify this point further, it should be understood that most agents operate in the knowledge that offering to represent an unpublished author may actually result in a lot of work that goes unpaid. This is in order to comply with the Association of Authors' Agents (AAA) code of practice, which states agents should not receive any monies for work carried out in relation to a manuscript until *the author* receives payment. (A stance in keeping with the traditional publishing model, in that the writer is not required to part with any money in order to see their book published.) Thus, any editorial development, career guidance and approach of commissioning editors are services given free of charge to an author with whom an agent has a representation agreement. It's only when an agent sells the rights to a book to a publisher that they receive money for their work, which comes in the form of a commission on royalties.

Yet the fear of failing to sell a manuscript shouldn't be interpreted as agents therefore being fixated on sales. It's realistic to acknowledge that securing deals for their list of clients is a priority but, for most, it's one offset by doing right by every individual author they represent. While it's a manuscript that brings a writer to their attention initially, an agent should see beyond the book in front of them and think long term. An agent will make it known their offer of representation is not just about being impressed by the manuscript you've approached them with, but that they believe in your ideas and your writing in such a way that they're prepared to invest their time and expertise into developing your next book, the one that follows and the one after that. Yes, their immediate task is to make sure Book One realises its potential and for them to secure rights deals with at least one publisher, but if this doesn't come to pass they'll continue to work with you on the next project.

So how can you, as our potential published author, begin submitting your work to prospective agents in a way that boosts your chance of gaining representation? By bearing these three key points in mind: having an appreciation of the corner of the market you're writing in; identifying the right agent for your book; and making sure your manuscript hits the spot.

# Do I need a literary agent to get published?

In the case of a non-fiction manuscript for either the academic or special interest market: no. Authors tend to be able to send these proposals to editors direct, and publishers' websites should offer guidelines to follow.

For writers of fiction or popular narrative non-fiction: yes. Some small presses do still operate an open submissions policy (again, check their guidelines if you've identified one as a good potential home for your book), but the vast majority of companies working within the traditional model of publishing won't even look at your work unless it's been sent to them by a literary agent. 'Traditional' in this context means that the financial burden of acquiring, producing and then selling a book is taken on entirely by the publisher. Thus, if sales are lower than expected – so much so that the book does not earn out the advance on royalties the publisher has already paid out to the author – then it is the publisher who takes the hit. As agents operate within the commercial side of the market, you can rest assured that these principles will apply to your book should you gain representation.

Having an agent does offer an author plenty of benefits, though:

- agents live and breathe contracts, making their clients far more likely to receive better terms. Having never seen a publishing contract before, there is little chance of an unrepresented writer being able to negotiate a better advance, better royalties, or have the wherewithal to secure rights deals in other territories, than an agent could;

- agents push authors further with their manuscript before sending it out to editors. They earmark editors as potential buyers and, having seen which books they've worked on and/or by having got to know them, have a good idea of the sort of narrative or book concept that will pique their interest;

- they know the market inside out and have a clear idea of and have a clear idea of how much you and your book are worth to a publisher;

- an agent acting on your behalf means that – crucially – you have more time to write.

The only way to be absolutely sure about whether or not a publisher considers unsolicited submissions is by reading their guidelines. The most recent edition of the *Writers' & Artists' Yearbook* is a great resource as it contains the general submission details for *all* reputable UK and Irish publishers, enabling you to narrow your search by getting an idea of the sorts of books their agents represent. Once you have a list of agencies, the next step is to double-check their guidelines by visiting their individual websites (with most containing agent-specific bios to read through as well).

---

## A NOTE ON SELF-PUBLISHING

It should be pointed out that a plausible way to go after commercial success without the guidance or representation of an agent is to self-publish. Huge improvements in, and availability of, digital technology have made this much easier to carry out and therefore a more attractive proposition to authors. Access to quality design options, availability of distribution channels, speed-to-market and also increased know-how in terms of being able to make a target audience aware of a book means the concept of self-publishing has come a long way and has become a viable way to begin a career as an author without agent representation. More recently, crowdfunding has become another route-to-market that has risen in popularity, and also does not require agent representation. Yet while there are certain examples – Hugh Howey's *Wool* from a self-publishing perspective, or the crowdfunded *The Madonna of Bolton* (Matt Cain) or *The Good Immigrant* (Nikesh Shukla) –

---

of books published in this way enjoying great success, authors going it alone should consider:

- you take on the responsibility for researching the company you're signing with, as well as understanding the agreement they offer. Do you know what's standard and what isn't? It's unlikely a company will blatantly pull the wool over the eyes of an unrepresented author (not least because things like standard royalty rates, for example, can be found with a bit of research) but by the same token a publisher has no need to make a contract anything other than weighted more in their favour than yours. You need to know how reasonable their proposed terms are, and not having an agent to turn to for guidance could lead to ill-informed decisions;

- no matter how prudent or savvy you think you are, it would be wise to become a member of either the Writers' Guild or the Society of Authors at this juncture. They won't fight for a better (or search for another) deal in the same way an agent would, but they do provide invaluable context around what you're agreeing to;

- no agent means no one takes commission on the royalties your book earns. Initially this might sound great, but in the long term is it actually worth it? Does the amount of commission an agent earns outweigh the value of their editorial guidance and the rights deals you probably couldn't negotiate (not to mention all of the admin they do on your behalf)? On the whole, a question to ask yourself is: do you want the *business side* of being a writer to impinge on your writing time?

If you have a work of non-narrative non-fiction published without an agent (which is more the norm) then it is also reasonable to assume your publisher will operate within these principles. For self-publishing or crowdfunding authors, however, the situation is obviously different. These books often require a form of financial investment ahead of being published. To have a book published by a crowdfunding platform means an author must convince people to offer financial backing. Without this target being hit a book won't go into production. And while feasible to self-publish a book for free, for it to reach a competitive market-standard an author is likely to need to pay for professional services. A cover designer may need to be employed, for example. How much money are you comfortable investing when there can be no guarantee of the number of copies your book will sell?

## What does a literary agent actually do?

In a nutshell, the job of a literary agent is to sell your manuscript to publishers and secure terms beneficial in both the short- and long-term life of your book. They understand you creatively and look to support and develop your career as a writer. Basically, agents act on your behalf by championing your book, brokering the best deal possible for it, and acting as a buffer between you and your publisher. They do the worrying so you can do the writing.

Broadly speaking, an agent's job can be broken down into three areas: **creative**, **business**, and **people-related**.

In a **creative** sense, an agent has to be in sync with what their writers are working towards and hone manuscripts so that they reach their potential ahead of going out to publishers. In being offered representation, you will have gained a passionate, influential supporter of your book and creative outlook in general. Agents may work through several versions of your manuscript with you ahead of sending it out to commissioning editors they have identified as potentially interested in bidding for the rights to your book. If the process of rewriting means tightening up character arcs, concentrating on giving your book more 'heart' or restructuring to create a pacier plot, then your agent will tell you straight. This requires you, the writer, to trust them and be willing to let go of your book enough to be guided by someone with your best interests at heart and an eye on what they *know* editors are looking for. Before approaching an agent you should have a reasonable  idea where your book would sit within a bookstore, and an agent will bring further genre-specific expertise to the table. As a result, they will push your work to a level they believe to be as market-ready as possible, and then send it out to commissioning editors.

This overarching appreciation of publishing as a commercial enterprise is where an agent's creative support meets their eye for **business**. Agents constantly have their ear to the ground for deals being done; the sorts of books editors are buying and where rights are being sold for particular books. This informs their strategy when it comes to approaching potential buyers of a manuscript, and also how much to push for during financial negotiations. All of which, of course, needs to be tied up contractually, and an agent's keen eye for small print is something that benefits their authors. It's the meat and potatoes of an agent's job to look into any sort of contractual query (financial or otherwise) and find solutions so that their authors are rewarded for their writing.

The third attribute of a literary agent complements both the creative and commercial elements of their role. Like most jobs in the Arts (and beyond!) being able to **relate to people** counts for a great deal. The business side of their job, for example, comes down to having good contacts. This requires acquiring up an understanding of what commissioning editors have on their wish-list, and this is built up over time through chance conversations and/or more formal meetings. These are the moments they can put forward manuscripts, either by planting a seed and mentioning how excited they are by a book one of their unpublished clients is putting finishing touches to, or by more seriously proclaiming a book to be ready and one an editor must read. As a yet-to-be published writer, this, as far as you're concerned, is the primary role of the agent; to champion your book and pitch it with such passion that an editor feels compelled to put everything else aside and read it. Whether it be in-person over a coffee or by email, an agent's ability to transfer their enthusiasm for your project is integral to their job and will open doors for your book.

Being able to relate to people is more than an agent being a good salesperson for their authors, though. There's a huge difference in approach between chasing royalty payments or interrogating the terms of a publishing agreement, for example, and speaking to an overwhelmed debut author suddenly stifled by 'imposter' syndrome. In fact, perhaps the greatest test of an agent's emotional dexterity is their handling of what brings the best out of their authors. Do they need 'tough love' and hard deadlines, or will they respond more to a sympathetic ear that coaxes them through a crisis of confidence?

## What don't agents do?

Literary agents don't write your book for you and they don't work for publishing houses. They also do not guarantee your book will get published, only that they will give everything they can to try to make it happen.

From a creative point of view, a literary agent interrogates your manuscript to make sure it's as tight as possible and teases out elements that could strengthen it further. Editorial work therefore comprises of whatever's deemed necessary to make your book ready to go out to editors, and varies from a straightforward copy-edit to scrutiny of entire story arcs and several rewrites. This exacting critique of your work might mean a lot of heavy-lifting on your part, but it's exactly what one should expect from the process once an agent has added you to their list of clients. An agent's job is to make sure your manuscript is at a publishable standard for the simple reason that editors might be put off by the amount of time they'd need to spend knocking the book into shape. It's common for several departments to read a book before it's acquired, making it vital that it's as polished as possible.

Agents don't work for publishers so have no allegiance to one publishing house over another. They may have better working relationships with certain editors, but sentiment is unlikely to get in the way when they have a vested interest in securing the best outcome for their author. Also, the fact that acquisitions are now decided by committee puts paid to the notion there can be bias towards a particular publisher just because an agent and an editor get on. Yes, the publisher might get a look at the book ahead of others (and the commissioning editor obviously plays an influential role because they essentially pitch the book to their colleagues), but if doubts are raised about investing in a book by the Sales and Marketing team, for example, a bid for the rights might not be made.

One other thing an agent doesn't want to do is interfere with the author–editor relationship. Once rights have been agreed and a publishing agreement signed, a relationship between the author and their editor should begin to get stronger. An agent will try to make space for this to happen, but this isn't to suggest they're not in touch with their author. They will keep an eye on key points in the publication process, and step in if queries arise or discussions need to be had. They are also likely to join their author to help influence meetings about cover-design options and marketing and publicity campaigns. In an ideal world, though, an author should hit it off with the people in-house working on their book and establish the same sort of positive relationship as they have with their agent, who, in the meantime, may well be working to secure an international or subsidiary rights deal with another publisher operating in a different territory.

## How do literary agents make money from my book?

On commission. A standard rate of commission an agent will charge upon selling the UK rights to your book is around 15 per cent, while you can expect an agent to charge a 20 per cent commission on either translation rights to a publisher in a different territory, or for negotiating the sale of film and TV rights. These are fairly standard figures but do check carefully when looking through the agencies listed within the *Writers' & Artists' Yearbook*. Here is an example based on your book being acquired by a UK publisher:

- you accept your agent's offer of representation;

- your agent suggests that improvements to your manuscript are needed and you spend a few months sending re-writes back and forth;

- your agent submits your manuscript to a publisher. They're interested and want UK and Commonwealth rights. They offer a £10,000 advance on royalties and agree that the writer takes 10 per cent of every sale after this has been earned out. (A bid for UK and Commonwealth rights is used to simplify this example but in reality a publisher may also bid for World rights too – a decision to be mulled over by your agent.);

- you discuss with your agent and decide to sign an agreement. Incrementally (likely to be paid out in three instalments: on signature, manuscript delivery, and on publication day) the publisher transfers £10,000 to your agent's agency account. This is the first time your book generates money, and is therefore the first time your agent takes commission for their involvement (so from the total of £10,000 advance on royalties, you receive 85 per cent [£8,500] and your agent takes 15 per cent [£1,500]). If your agent sells the rights to your book to a publisher outside of the UK, this same process is repeated, except the percentage per sale kept by the publisher could be higher or lower, and your agent will take in the region of 20 per cent commission;

- neither author nor agent receive further monies in relation to the book *until* royalties exceed the £10,000 advance initially paid out by the publisher. This means 10 per cent on every copy sold goes towards paying off the advance.

Once enough copies of the book have been sold to earn out the advance of £10,000, 10 per cent of every sale beyond this figure reverts to the author–agent split (85 per cent:15 per cent). So if total royalties from sales accumulated are £30,000, the publisher would deduct the royalties already received (£10,000), then pay the remaining £20,000. The author would take 85 per cent (£17,000) and the agent would take the remaining 15 per cent (£3,000).

The majority of agents earn a base salary (unless they work for themselves), with the royalties they bring in from each author going to their agency account. All authors need to know is that their agent makes no money from them and that their services are entirely free until a publisher pays the first instalment of their advance on royalties. The financial incentive an agent works towards is therefore closely aligned to the wishes of the authors they represent: to go out and find the right deal for their book.

SEE ALSO *What's an author advance?* page 213 and *How do agents get paid?* page 216.

## Will I make more money per sale without an agent?

Unless you somehow possess a fair amount of knowledge around publishing contracts, operating without an agent means negotiating rights and royalties with a publisher is left to you. Are there positives to accepting a more modest advance from a smaller publisher (i.e. they can't afford to compete with a bigger company but will make your book one of their leading titles if you publish with them; you'll begin receiving royalties quicker) or are you about to agree terms with a publisher which, in paying out a relatively small advance on royalties, doesn't need to work that hard to make their money back? Do you have the contacts that would help you sell the rights to your book to publishers in different territories? Or would it be better to sell global rights to a single publisher?

Yes, in theory not having an agent does mean you retain 100 per cent of the royalties you agree with your publisher. In practice, though, how good will the deal you end up with actually be? First, if you publish fiction or narrative non-fiction, your chances of being traditionally published reduce without an agent. And second, even though it *is* possible to be published in the traditional manner by a smaller press, it's highly likely an agent would have negotiated better terms. So instead of thinking about 'losing out' on the 15 per cent commission an agent charges on your royalties, consider the larger advances, more favourable terms and the potential for more than one rights deal you might miss out on by not being represented.

Authors who self-publish successfully do stand to make more on a per-sale basis. This is because they retain a much bigger slice of the pie, giving away nothing more than a comparatively small percentage per-sale to the platform that lists and/or prints and distributes the book. This, along with speed-to-market, complete creative freedom and autonomy over the entire publishing process means some authors have found the self-publishing model a very attractive one, although the challenge of project management and the potential expense of marketing and publicity to give a book a chance to find a readership are huge caveats that tend to ward off initial enthusiasm.

## Do agents just care about sales figures?

It's negative and overly simplistic to assume literary agents care about nothing more than sales. Ultimately, yes, an agent charges commission on royalties and are held to account by the business they bring in but money cannot be their major motivator. In order to successfully fend off rival offers of representation for an author, to pitch passionately to publishers and to sell the rights to books, agents *have* to connect emotionally with the writing and their author on some level. How can they expect to be creatively in tune with what their authors are trying to achieve, or have a good sense of what's coming next in terms of the sort of books editors are looking for, by concentrating purely on financial return?

This is not to say, of course, that agents who secure big deals are to be treated with suspicion. If you've got a commercial book with a great hook or which has been written about a subject that suddenly taps into the zeitgeist, healthy sales could follow. Reasons for books selling well tend to be a blend of talent and timing, although the emotional intelligence and commercial savvy of an agent is also likely to have been an important factor. In understanding you and your writing, an agent will have prioritised sending your book to the right editor working for a publisher with a track record of publishing your type of book well. This sort of decision is unlikely to have been just about sales, because those in the industry know there can be no guarantee they will follow in the numbers you hope for; it is, though, about an agent doing the right thing for your book, and sometimes that can lead to bestsellers being born.

## What is an agent's typical working day?

There's no way of providing a definitive answer to this question because the day-to-day demands on an agent can be so varied. A single working day could consist of anything from:

- pre-representation meetings with writers who are prospective clients;
- contracts on an author-by-author basis. Authors are likely to have more than one deal linked to their book, so sorting out the paperwork can take up a lot of time and will range from negotiation through to chasing the signatures required;
- chasing money: are royalty statements (usually issued twice a year) on time, are they correct and has the money appeared in the agency account? Have invoices been raised/paid?
- meetings with editors at publishers. What are they looking to acquire? Which books does an agent have that might be of interest to them?
- calls and/or emails from different departments at a publisher (rights, publicity, editorial);

- editorial work on the latest draft of a manuscript;
- preparing a submission to an editor on behalf of a client;
- seeking out other rights opportunities in other markets, such as film & TV, audio or translation;
- appearing as a speaker at a writing or publishing event;
- speaking to literary scouts;
- attending a book launch (either for one of the authors they represent or as a networking opportunity);
- speaking to existing clients about edits and/or to offer reassurance regarding the way a manuscript is developing;
- going to an industry event, such as an award ceremony;
- discussions with an author around decisions or requests made by their publisher;
- emails, social media, and other office admin.

You may have noticed one crucial omission from this list. Agents find it increasingly difficult to dedicate time within office working hours to reading *unsolicited* manuscript submissions. The majority of agents read these either on the go, before or after work, or over the weekend, which is why it's so important that unsolicited manuscripts stick to agency guidelines. Following these means you present your writing in a way agents find easiest to focus on your opening chapters. Ask yourself this: do your words do enough to hold their attention during time that might otherwise be spent with family, friends, walking the dog or watching a box set?

## How do agents become agents?

There are two general routes to becoming an agent: either through having worked at an agency following a placement or internship and being promoted from within, or after working in another part of the publishing industry (usually in editorial or rights) and deciding on a change in career path.

Entry level roles at an agency tend to be as a reader and an assistant to an established agent. These provide good exposure to developing an eye for spotting talent, an understanding of the market, and eventually absorbing lessons around negotiation, contracts, rights to push for and the general subtleties of the job. Invaluable industry contacts are also likely to be gathered as par for the course. The significant next step for a 'junior agent' comes in managing to juggle their existing responsibilities with finding, taking on and working to develop the manuscripts of clients of their own. These are the beginnings of an agent forming their own list of authors.

People that move into agenting after holding a job in publishing might not have agency-specific know-how to begin with but do have a solid understanding of the industry and bring other strengths to the table. For example, a background in editorial could be invaluable in being able to take on unpolished debut writers and help manuscripts meet their potential, while a previous role in rights obviously makes for an agent with an eye for contractual small print and lots of contacts.

SEE ALSO *Should I submit to a new or more established agent?* page 90.

## Do literary agents 'head-hunt' authors?

Sometimes, particularly if your writing has won or been shortlisted for a competition/award or, particularly where non-fiction is concerned, you have shown yourself to have a profile or a unique take on a subject with potential for a book. Are you involved in a story that's in the news, for example, or have you become a prominent voice as a result of a blog or social media activity?

Some agents can be active on the creative writing circuit too, speaking at events, being part of judging panels or providing students with feedback on their writing. This raises their profile among writers actively working on manuscripts but has the added benefit of perhaps unearthing new talent.

On the whole, though, the chances of this happening are quite slim. Being proactive and submitting to select agents provides the best chance of representation.

## Do I need an agent if ...

Here are some quick-fire answers to a variety of scenarios that can leave authors wondering whether they need an agent or not.

### ... I WRITE NON-FICTION?

It depends what type of non-fiction. If you write narrative-led non-fiction (such as memoir or biography) then chances are you *will* need an agent. If you write non-narrative non-fiction (recipes, pop culture, journalism, politics, history, etc.) then, as the aim is still likely to sell in the commercial marketplace, it might not always be necessary to have an agent, but you'll get a better deal if you do. If you're writing non-narrative non-fiction for a more specialised audience (such as an instructional book or an academic study), you'll probably be able to approach publishers direct.

### ... I'VE ALREADY SELF-PUBLISHED?

The jury is out on this. Some agents may be of the mind that unless sales are huge, they're unlikely to be interested in a book that's already been self-published. Why would a publisher want a book that's already gone out into the market? And has it already reached the entirety of its target audience? That being said, some agents view things differently. If a self-published title appeals to them but it hasn't sold in huge numbers, it could well be that their assistance in negotiating a deal with a publisher who can get the book in 'bricks and mortar' retailers and commit to marketing and publicity campaigns, could help the book go on to sell a more significant number of copies. (The author does need to be willing to take down the self-published version of the book from other retail sites in this case, though.)

### ... I'M AN ILLUSTRATOR?

In general, no: most illustrators develop their own set of contacts and get commissions through people looking at their online portfolio. However, if you want to be commissioned to illustrate a book that a publisher has invested money in, then yes. Children's literary agents do represent authors *and* illustrators, while there are obviously standalone agents for illustrators too.

### ... I'M A GRAPHIC NOVELIST?

As with illustrators, agent representation comes with advantages (someone to look at rights and contracts, to help find regular work) but it's not immediately necessary. Graphic novelists can often submit to magazines and publishers direct, while they're able to showcase and grow an audience for their work online.

### ... I'M A POET?

Poets tend not to have agents unless they also write prose – a much larger and potentially more profitable business for an agent to work in than the relatively small and non-commercial poetry community. To begin having their work published, poets tend to submit to poetry websites, competitions, magazines and journals, while every now and again opportunities can also arise that are a little more commercial, such as an advertising company or a particular brand looking for poetry.

### ... I WRITE SHORT STORIES?

Short story anthologies tend not to sell in great numbers so, while an agent may offer representation off the strength of a writer pitching a collection of work in this form, it can be difficult for an agent to woo a commissioning editor unless there is a novel in the pipeline too.

## How many clients does an agent represent?

This is an impossible question to answer for several reasons: some agencies don't list authors against their agents' names online; some agents only list published authors against their name; and some – perhaps lesser established – agents might list authors yet to have signed a deal with a publisher.

In terms of the typical number of *published* clients an agent represents, again this can vary depending on personality, assistance (agency readers, an assistant or a contracts manager to delegate certain tasks to) and how much time an agent likes to work with their authors editorially. The type of writer an agent represents is also a factor. Assuming an agent works for a small agency and has ten published clients, if they all write genre fiction (crime, romance, writing for children), the market expectation would be for them to publish books fairly regularly. This would produce more than enough work (multiple rights deals, royalty agreements, editorial work, etc.) to keep an agent busy. If, however, an agent represents ten literary fiction authors, their output would be unlikely to be as prolific, meaning they may feel they can add more authors to their list.

# Literary agents and the publishing industry

Literary agents have become an integral part of the broader industry landscape that keeps the traditional model of publishing ticking over. Agents – rather than publishers' in-house editorial teams – sift through unsolicited submissions for gold; they develop then deliver new writing talent to editors; they work with teams across the full spectrum of the publishing process; and they negotiate better terms for their writers, as well as spot new opportunities for them to make money from their book.

It might not please the purist, but modern publishers are now expected to be so much more than simply a place dedicated to editing and producing books. Many publishers cannot afford large editorial departments in-house (a situation unlikely to change with supermarkets and online retailers driving down retail prices), and editors' further responsibilities mean they may have much less time than ever to spend looking at text. It has therefore become a necessity for agents to take the burden of assessing unsolicited submissions for talent, and this works as a helpful filter for publishers, who know any unpublished manuscript referred to their department is from an agent and therefore of a high standard.

One knock-on effect of publishers needing to guard against the increasing competition books face in terms of being a product modern-day consumers want to buy, is a more holistic approach to deciding which new titles they invest in. Books are no longer acquired on the say-so of a single editor. Instead, an editor has to passionately present a book in an acquisitions meeting to a committee of people from editorial, sales, rights and marketing, some of whom will go away and read the manuscript. With this knowledge in mind, agents know that for their unpublished client to have the slightest chance of being acquired, their manuscript needs to be as editorially sound as possible upon submission. The 'heavy-lifting' of manuscript edits, therefore, now also lies at the door of the literary agent.

In short, agents enjoy a significant influence on the publishing food chain. Commissioning editors want to know them because they know they're only going to serve up manuscripts written to a good standard and tailored to their literary tastes. And writers want to know them because they provide the best chance of their book being bought and published.

## What does a publisher do?

Publishing companies are commercial enterprises. They acquire the rights to an author's manuscript then pour the necessary resources into it becoming a book. Names one might associate with long established publishers are Penguin Random House, HarperCollins, Faber & Faber and Bloomsbury. Although smaller independent presses may operate an open submissions policy, in the main publishers of fiction and popular non-fiction do not accept unsolicited manuscripts, meaning writers cannot make a direct approach for publication. Authors of non-narrative non-fiction (non-fiction books that are not memoir, autobiography or biography) for a more specialist audience may be able to send a proposal for editors to consider, though (with agent representation not a requirement).

## Do publishers ever approach unpublished authors?

Yes, but only in quite particular circumstances and most likely in relation to non-fiction. If you are a celebrity, a leading industry voice or a journalist heavily involved in the reporting of something that has captured the public interest, a publisher may make a direct approach to see if you might be interested in writing a book.

## How does working directly with a publisher change things for the author?

In the main, working with a publisher without being represented by an agent shouldn't alter the nuts-and-bolts process of a book being produced. They've invested some of their acquisitions budget in you, so want your book to be a success. Editorial discussions will still happen and marketing and publicity campaigns will be discussed, all with the best interests of the book at heart: agent or no agent.

The thing is, what happens if there are bumps in the road? Who do you turn to if you don't agree with something suggested, or fully understand something you're asked to do? And then there's the subject of rights and royalties stated in your publishing agreement. Can you be sure a publisher has offered terms that work as well as for you as they should?

An agent not only knows your book's worth, but they are also financially incentivised to care about it because it means they earn more from the commission they charge. It's their bread and butter to check contracts, to think about rights with more than one publisher, and to consider opportunities for your writing outside of publishing too. Even if you sign to a publisher without an agent and you're happy with the terms agreed and everything they do to edit, produce and publicise your book, it's unlikely for their hard-working rights team (stretched across many other books) to be able to offer the same service.

## How do agents and publishers work together?

It's very much worth the while of both agents and editors to develop a good working relationship because, to a certain extent, they rely on one another to succeed. Agents recommend manuscripts to editors that are of a high quality and complementary to the list of titles they already publish. Commissioning editors, meanwhile, hold the keys to the door of a publishing house, and all of the finance and resources they are able to put towards turning a writer's manuscript into a book that competes in the marketplace. The job of an agent is to persuasively pitch the work of their clients to commissioning editors, who in turn (provided they love it and believe they can publish it well), will pick up the baton and champion the book in an acquisitions meeting, hoping to convince their colleagues the book is a worthwhile investment and that they should make the money available to bid for rights.

As noted previously, once an author signs a publishing agreement with a publisher, they usually receive an advance on royalties, and then further royalties provided when sales generated surpass the figure of the advance. An agent charges their author commission in either instance. This rate of commission in no way impacts the percentage per-sale a publisher takes home from each book sold so, once an agent's client has a deal with a publisher, theoretically an agent shouldn't really need to have much contact with them. This is not the way it works in practice, though. Editors are the main point of contact for agents, who continue to keep an eye on things as the book goes through the publishing process. Acting on behalf of their authors doesn't mean just finding a deal, it means they are on hand to offer advice or answer questions, have their say on publicity schedules and cover design options, and sign off things like press releases or cover copy.

## How do agents know which commissioning editors to target?

A major aspect of a literary agent's job is getting to know editors who could acquire the books of their authors. Both parties, therefore, make it their business to arrange meetings where an agent can talk about the projects their clients are working on, and editors can provide insight into the sort of things they're looking to acquire and how they're hoping to develop their list in general. This (or even a more informal chat at a book launch or an industry event) is a perfect opportunity for an agent to whet an editor's appetite by using that short, memorable one-line pitch for your book you've both worked on, something that might not seem of great significance when you first came up with it, but which now should plant a seed in the mind of an editor where your book is concerned, heightening anticipation ahead of it being submitted to them.

One other advantage an agent can gain from having a good relationship with an editor is that it can sometimes give them the inside track on job changes or decisions made in terms of a new direction for a list. Could this lead to an opportunity for one of their writers? Or could being tipped off about these changes save them time and lead to them concentrating on finding a deal elsewhere?

## Who edits my book: an agent or an editor?

You have to be prepared for both to edit your book. If your manuscript is considered 'submission-ready' by your agent, then happy days. Most debut writers, however, are likely to be in the position of having a manuscript that's imperfect but with real potential. If an agent offers to represent you, they do so in the knowledge they need to help polish that rough diamond into something an editor can't refuse. Their involvement should help you improve your book.

However, once a book is acquired by a publisher it's extremely likely that more edits lie in wait. Most manuscripts undergo at least one in-house edit, with these notes from your editor going across to your agent who will run through them with you. In an ideal world, nothing too contentious would arise at this stage, but realistically a publishing house editor won't allow sentiment to get in the way of making changes they believe will improve a book, be that a change of title, cutting a prologue or recommending a character is culled. Suggested major changes like these are ones to be discussed with your agent. Emotions aside, is there a good reason for what your editor is suggesting?

Or perhaps you have a solution you'd like to propose. Here, an agent's role as a mediator – guiding, reassuring and fighting your corner as necessary – can become invaluable to your ongoing relationship with your publisher.

For writers of non-narrative non-fiction manuscripts, however, it's likely that the primary editorial relationship will be with the editor at their publisher. This is simply because their manuscript will not have needed to be finished ahead of their book being acquired (although at least one sample chapter will have been submitted, and a thorough chapter breakdown agreed too). This means from the full first draft onwards, the author will send their work directly to the in-house editor responsible for taking their book through to production.

SEE ALSO *Do I need to finish my manuscript before submitting?* page 57.

## How long does it take for a book to be published?

From the point of the book being sold to a publisher, it can take generally between twelve and eighteen months for that title to hit the shops, although authors can experience a longer or shorter lead time depending on how their book fits into pre-existing schedules. A publisher could also purposefully hold a book back to coincide with a noteworthy date, or rush one into production to try and capitalise on a surge of public interest in a subject that's been in the news of late.

Note that estimate is *not* from the moment a writer starts working on their book, *not* from the point a book is sent out to agents, and *not* from when an agent makes an offer of representation. After a writer has an agent, a manuscript could either be sent out to tender very quickly or subjected to two or three redrafts, slowing things down by several months. A period of waiting may also need to be endured when an agent puts a manuscript out on submission with editors. Response-time could be within twenty-four hours or, depending on how often acquisitions meetings are held, it could take a couple of months – frustrating for a writer who has come so far with their book.

## What are sales like in my section of the marketplace?

This is something worth considering as your manuscript nears being ready to send out to prospective agents. Unfortunately, hard figures are difficult to get hold of without access to something like a Nielsen Bookscan account, while going by any figures printed as part of bestseller charts might inflate rather than ground your sales expectations.

It's definitely useful to do a bit of digging, though. To start with, you should be an avid reader of contemporary books in your genre. This not only gives you an idea of what sells, but will also help you understand where your book sits in relation to others. Readers of which other contemporary author might be interested in reading your book? What does your book do that's a bit different? Why should people pick your book over the others vying for their attention?

Next, searching online for in-depth articles on recent trends and subscribing to a publishing industry magazine like *The Bookseller* will provide you with useful insight on books acquired, perhaps by agents you've earmarked to submit your manuscript to. This sort of reading is also a good way to get an objective take on the general market/reader demand for your type of book.

While there's always going to be a genre-busting sensation that unexpectedly breaks through (see the transformative effect *Fifty Shades of Grey* had on sales of erotic novels), you should be able to draw general conclusions about the market demand for your book. Crime thrillers are perennial favourites and can sell well, for example, but there is a huge amount of competition). Are YA trilogies as in demand as they once were, though? And does this mean fewer publishers are going to show an interest in taking on your book as a result?

Don't get too bogged down in the latest market trends or become too invested in how well *other* books are selling, though. The important things are to be well read in the corner of the market you want to enter, and have a general appreciation of how the business side of publishing works. To chase the market is a mistake that leaves authors coming up short creatively, so stick to writing in a way that works for you.

# The author–agent relationship: finding a literary agent

Given that the majority of publishers of fiction and popular non-fiction no longer have to read the hundreds of unsolicited manuscript submissions sent in weekly by unrepresented writers, they are also no longer charged with being the people that say No. Rejection letters are now, in the main, the burden of the literary agent.

While agents want to hear from writers and open manuscript submissions genuinely hoping that they're good (they're reliant upon great new writing to put food on the table!), the knuckle-clenching truth aspiring authors have to face is that competition is fierce and the standard high. It can be very difficult to gain representation.

Be in no doubt that the number of agents working in your part of the market is dwarfed by the number of writers pitching book ideas to them. Agents are therefore very selective (out of necessity, but also to protect their reputation with editors) about the writers they decide to take on. If a manuscript is not ready or not within the bounds of the genres they typically represent, then they will pass up the chance to represent it.

However, most agents will explain that many of the rejections they send out are due to authors not having done some basic research into the types of books and writers those agents are actively looking for. So even before we come to the fundamental question that every writer must ask ahead of sending their submission out – 'Is My Manuscript Ready?' – this section focuses on how dedicating time to researching potential agents can immediately pay dividends. And why wouldn't you want to do this? If the person you're approaching to act on your behalf is going to be charging 15–20 per cent commission on your royalties and become responsible for taking your book to prospective publishers, then surely it's worth your while? Would you buy a house, book a hotel or even go and see a film without doing a bit of background research? True, this sort of information might not be as handily compiled, but it definitely isn't inaccessible either – much of it will be available online – and given the amount of time and effort you've put into writing your manuscript, what are another couple of hours? When you're considering an agent, look at which writers they represent. Can you get an idea of their background (editorial, rights, marketing)? Are they actually accepting submissions at the moment? Have they expressed the sort of books they're really on the lookout for (maybe as a Twitter wish-list)? What are their submission guidelines? These sorts of details could prove crucial and should therefore go hand-in-hand with the process of fine-tuning your manuscript and readying it for submission.

## How do I start to look for an agent?

For over a century, the *Writers' & Artists' Yearbook* has been the go-to resource for writers looking for publishing industry information, and that it still sells in its thousands marks it out as the essential reference tool. Each section of the *Yearbook* comes with articles that provide useful context on a variety of topics: writing advice, reviews of recent publishing trends, and insights from industry professionals. Accompanying these articles is a curated list of contact details, and within the literary agencies section there are details about submission guidelines, individual agent names, and the genres of book an agency is looking for. Publishers, agencies, competitions, prizes and more included within the Listings section are vetted by the *Yearbook*'s team of editors each year, and where literary agencies are concerned, the book lists members and non-members of the Association of Authors' Agents (AAA) but does not knowingly include anyone charging a reading fee. Over the years, the *Yearbook* has been the diving board from which many a now-recognised author has stood to assess the water before diving into more detailed research on who their book might appeal to.

Twitter has also become a brilliant place to start looking for literary agents, and has the added benefit of being able to offer a bit more of an insight into their personality and what they're reading right now. Most agent's Twitter profiles will state which agency they work for, and include either their individual submissions email address, or a link to their agency submission guidelines. Looking at the other people an agent follows on Twitter is another useful thing to browse, as these could be other agents or writers that could be of interest to you.

Using Twitter as a resource will probably lead you to clicking through to agency websites, and a bit of general internet browsing of agencies is another good use of your time. This can be more targeted if you're confident about the genre of your book (e.g. search: 'Literary agents UK crime and thriller'). This might also bring up videos, podcasts or written interviews in which an agent gives further insight into the sort of writing that appeals to them.

Finally, if you're a reader of contemporary books published within the genre you're writing (which you really should be …) then taking a look at the Acknowledgements section at the front/back of books can be a great way to seek out agents that represent authors you see as being peers. You can't guarantee an agent will always be name-checked but thanks is often given, and from this you should be able to search online to find out who else they represent, what their submission guidelines are, etc.

## Do agents specialise in specific areas?

Absolutely, and they will state exactly what they're looking for on their agency website page. Some, however, will be more prescriptive than others, which can be interpreted by authors as either a cause of frustration, or as an opportunity. Agent A, for example, may state 'I'm looking for literary fiction told with a unique voice', while

Agent B would like 'high-action adventure for young adults, ideally involving cyber crime and/or climate change'. Furthermore, Agent B goes on to state what they do *not* want to read: 'I do not consider books with a supernatural element or with protagonists that are animals.'

In the examples above, Agent A has deliberately kept their submission criteria quite broad (perhaps to extend the range of authors they represent), while Agent B has decided to restrict the submissions coming in to them by being very specific. This is why taking care to do research is so worthwhile, because agents should be considered specialists within certain broader areas. Where non-fiction is concerned, for example, it's quite normal for particular topics (say politics, history and current affairs) to be specified as clear areas of interest even though they technically fit within the broader label of adult non-fiction. Writers of children's fiction and non-fiction should also look at this carefully, paying attention to the age range an agent represents. There's a big difference, for example, between an agent representing picture book authors and writers who publish work in the middle-grade (8–11 years) category.

SEE ALSO *What type of book have I written?* page 36.

## How do I know if an agent is right for me?

You probably won't truly know the answer to this until you meet them, but by doing some research into what sort of writing an agent is looking for, and looking through the authors they currently represent, you can at least get an indication of whether you're going to see eye-to-eye in terms of writing style and/or genre. Some agents are also willing to offer a glimpse into their non-work life on social media too, as noted above, with Twitter being the most natural home for writers and publishing industry professionals. Maybe you share a passion for cats? Perhaps you see the same way as them politically, you're obsessed with the same TV show or felt the same way about a much-hyped book published recently. Or maybe they've vented at the lack of stories narrated by sophisticated female psychopaths … and that's *exactly* the sort of book you've just written. All of this information may well mean everything or nothing in relation to your book, but could at least help decide whether to submit your work to someone or not.

If you submit your book proposal to an agent and they're intrigued enough to want to read more, then they'll contact you to ask for the full manuscript. This could be over the phone or by email, and a request that's likely to come with a window into what they like about your opening pages. In turn, this should provide a bit more of an insight into their personality, and also whether they share the same creative vision for your book as you do. All of which, of course, can be a help in gaining a better assessment of whether an agent is right for you. If an agent reads your full manuscript and makes you an offer of representation, wherever possible you should try to meet them in person ahead of signing an agreement, as this probably remains the best way to get a handle on how you might work together.

SEE ALSO *What sort of things should I ask if I meet a literary agent?* page 184.

## How do I know my writing is suited to my target market?

As much as your manuscript might contain a good idea and be tight structurally (both big ticks for a prospective agent), if your writing isn't appropriate for the market (language, style, etc.) in which you're hoping to compete, then consider your chances hampered.

Getting to know your corner of the marketplace comes down to reading as much as possible. Be an expert in your field and place your work against that of others to see where it fits in. Does your book offer a slightly different twist on what's been successful for Debut Author X, for example? Take it as a given that any agent you query with your work is an avid reader, so these are exactly the same sorts of questions they will be asking in relation to your manuscript. Why not give yourself a head-start and start asking them yourself beforehand?

So a solid appreciation of the market doesn't just have a significant bearing on which agents you query, but on the writing process itself. Don't just read for pleasure but start to treat emerging novelists in your section of the bookshop as contemporaries and read analytically. What are the things that do (or don't!) make a book work? Does your book follow a similar structure? Or if not, why not? Why are you emotionally invested in their characters? If you've deliberately moved away from something readers might come to expect, is this something that sets your book apart or the reason that it's faltering? An exhaustive knowledge of the type of book you're writing means you're more likely to confront, iron out and/or *own* the quirks of your own writing. It's a mirror to hold up to your work and help assess what your manuscript does well, differently, or where it needs improvement; having this awareness is vital if you're to make progress and either rewrite or submit.

Besides reading as much as possible to try to match the expert knowledge of your genre possessed by the agents you're approaching, another useful way to get to know the contemporary marketplace is by reading industry publications. Subscribing to *The Bookseller* or signing up to other industry newsletter bulletins can help you find out what's happening in the wider publishing world. Literary agents and commissioning editors spend a lot of their time reading manuscripts that end up taking two years to reach the public. As a result, there's every chance that they are a couple of steps ahead of current trends (which they helped shape in the first place), so paying attention to industry news means you're more on the inside track in terms of what's being bought. New hires are also reported on, as agents are recruited or move between companies etc. It's fair to assume they'll be looking to grow their list of authors, and the sort of writing they're interested in will be mentioned as part of this. Could it be an opportunity for your manuscript?

Finally, the best way to get an idea of whether your writing hits the mark and you have a book that will appeal to your intended readership is to simply give it to readers. If you're going to be a writer then you need your writing to be read, and if you can make those first readers people that form part of your target audience, so much the better. As a children's writer, have those in the age bracket you're hoping to appeal to given you their thoughts? If you're writing historical fiction, have you asked a couple of people who regularly read in the genre (and perhaps more importantly, people with a good knowledge of the specific historical period your book covers) for their opinion? It *is* scary and you'll need to be sure they'll neither sugarcoat nor destroy all confidence with the feedback they offer, but chances are your manuscript will emerge stronger once you've digested what they've had to say. Has their objective take pointed out something you'd previously been blind to? Are you able to find solutions to a criticism they had? Did they like something you feel you could go away and make more of? And are there consistencies in the feedback you've received from a couple of people? Not only will this prove a useful exercise in assessing whether your writing is on the money for your target market, it also identifies things to rework ahead of sending your book out on submission to agents: a group of readers who will definitely cut to the chase in terms of what works and what doesn't in your writing.

SEE ALSO *Should I show people my book before I submit?* page 54.

## What type of book have I written?

Many writers can be quite embarrassed to admit they perhaps don't really know how they would categorise their book. Is it romance, or historical fiction? Is it for a middle-grade readership or for young adults? Perhaps genre wasn't of great concern as part of the first draft (because you were concentrating on getting the story down on paper) and now the book falls between two stools, making it problematic to pitch the manuscript and submission to prospective agents. Ask yourself:

- is your book fiction or non-fiction? If it's fiction, then it will feature characters you have devised. This remains the case if you inhabit a character from history or your book plays out within real-life happenings (see Don DeLillo's *Libra* or Hilary Mantel's *Wolf Hall*). If your writing is a straightforward retelling of events, this is non-fiction (specifically memoir, biography or autobiography);

- if you're writing for children, is the language and content of your book appropriate for the age group you're aiming for?

- if you've written something you believe could genuinely qualify as more than one genre, while this could turn out to be a unique selling point ('USP') of the book in the end – publishers are always looking for titles with potential to become 'crossover' hits, as broader market appeal could mean bigger sales – when it comes to pitching to agents, you might need to pick a side. Which is the most dominant genre? Or are you classifying your book within a genre unnecessarily? For example, historical fiction novels often require a romance or crime element to help bring suspense and purpose to the narrative. To describe *Captain Corelli's Mandolin* as a piece of historical fiction would technically be accurate, but in doing so would also do a major disservice to the driving force of the book, which is that it's a love story.

If you're having doubts about where your book fits in with the genres displayed on Amazon or in a bookstore, you'll be relieved to know you're not the only one. It's quite common for agents to receive submissions from writers who haven't attached the right label to their book, and from time to time publishing editors and agents can disagree on where a book should be placed, too. This is largely because genre labels, while handy terms to group books together, are subject to opinion. Classifying a book as 'commercial' or 'literary', for example, is one that often divides opinion. Again, though, becoming an expert in your field by reading widely and keeping an eye on industry trends and terminology should prevent you from straying too far, and could prove to be a real advantage when it comes to pitching your book.

While using a genre label to describe your book is obviously useful, if you still find it challenging, you could always try comparing your book to another. This can make up part of your covering letter, and is a good way of helping the agent about to read your opening chapters get an immediate flavour for what to expect. Are there other writers, particular books, or even TV shows or films that have inspired your writing and you see a kinship with? Referencing these is a valid way to skirt around using a genre term you don't feel is quite appropriate, and performs exactly the same job as a framing device.

SEE ALSO *Blurb, pitch, elevator pitch, synopsis ... what's the difference?* page 110 and *The Covering Letter: comparisons* page 119.

## Why is genre important?

Genre terms work for booksellers because they're quick and understandable signposts. They bring order to the thousands of books vying for the attention of readers, streamlining them into sections they might be interested in. Supermarkets, which would become hugely frustrating places for shoppers if the mass of available items were not grouped into aisles of broadly related products, use exactly the same sort of system. Trends such as 'vampire teen fiction' or 'misery memoir' obviously come and go, but as a writer you should be familiar with the wider terms booksellers use to categorise (e.g. 'Crime & Thriller', 'Science Fiction', 'Historical Fiction').

Whilst knee-deep in a first draft, genre categorisation perhaps shouldn't overly concern you. But as soon as you begin thinking about sending your book off to agents, it's wise to start thinking more carefully about which shelf your book is going to sit on. First, as a tool for reference: What are the books similar to yours like? Are you approaching that level of writing? Is your story too similar to another book that's recently sold well? Knowing how your work might appeal to readers that have lapped up similar books means you can approach re-writing with this in mind, and also target agents that represent those authors.

And by the way, if you can't shift that nagging thought telling you not to conform to any of this because you don't want your book reduced to a mere label ('My writing shouldn't be pigeon-holed under a blanket term like "romance"'), look at it another way. No one's going to have the chance to realise the different textures of your book if they can't find it on a shelf. Only once your book is in the hands of a reader are you able to confound their expectations: your sweeping romance set against a hitherto unknown British political coup; your crime novel that unmasks the fractured psyche of a global icon. One of the key aspects of successful books is they meet reader expectations, and then subvert them. But you can't do this unless you entice that reader in the first place.

## What's the difference between literary and commercial fiction?

At what point in the process is it decided that a book should be classified as 'literary fiction', 'commercial fiction', or something that merges the two ('literary-commercial crossover' or 'book club fiction')?

Stereotypically, literary novels contain beautiful prose led by the bigger picture of the development of either character or theme, with plot (arguably) secondary. On a book-by-book basis, they also tend not to sell in as large a number as commercial fiction titles, though if the concept for a literary book is strong and the characters intriguing then, assisted by stellar reviews and nominations for some of the more established literary awards, big sales can follow (see recognised works from authors such as Kazuo Ishiguro, Deborah Levy and Ian McEwan for proof of this). Commercial fiction titles are often dismissed as plot-driven beasts with little subtlety in the writing, churned out to a formula defined by what works for the audience they're looking to serve. Yet a lot of the more successful books of recent times actually tend to blur the literary and commercial dividing lines. David Nicholls' *One Day*, Gillian Flynn's *Gone Girl* and Gail Honeyman's *Eleanor Oliphant Is Completely Fine* were all marketed as 'commercial' fiction but actually went on to appeal to readers of literary fiction. The same can be said of books positioned as 'literary', with Sarah Perry's *The Essex Serpent*, Jessie Burton's *The Miniaturist* and Sally Rooney's *Normal People* all great examples of literary novels that caught the imagination of the general reading public.

Chances are not one of the authors mentioned above wrote their book concerned by whether their book would be labelled as 'commercial' or 'literary'. And nor should you. However, when it comes to *pitching* your work, agents tend to be clear about which type of book they're looking for, and you need to be aware of how, if you are offered representation, this decision could set the course for the way your book goes on to be published. This is where knowing the market and having a clear idea of what your own manuscript does and doesn't do is crucial to deciding on the agents you approach. Is your book a straightforward psychological thriller full of end-of-chapter cliffhangers? Or is it a lyrical comment on our times viewed through the eyes of a young immigrant who has just arrived on UK shores? The agents you choose to approach with either of these novels are likely to affect how it's published, so researching them is key.

# Should I base my writing around what people are buying now?

Having an appreciation of trends could provide useful context in relation to your book, but never write to serve them. You won't necessarily enjoy what you're doing, and chances are you're destined to fall short, too. Assume every just-published book has taken two years at a minimum to become available to readers, meaning trends you're aware of right now probably aren't going to last the length of time it takes for you to get a manuscript written, represented, edited, re-edited and published. And even if that doesn't prove to be the case, wouldn't writing what you want to write make for a more enjoyable experience than jumping on someone else's bandwagon?

# What if my book is impossible to categorise?

This is unlikely. If you make this claim then, broadly speaking, there are three possible answers:

1.  you've not read enough. Even if your book doesn't neatly fit into a particular genre, it's seriously unlikely to be completely incomparable to the work of another writer, either thematically, stylistically or in relation to the story arc of your main character. Remember, in pitching your book to agents you're writing to absolutely avid readers of the particular genres they work in, leading most to treat such a claim as a personal challenge to prove you wrong;

2.  you actually *have* written something that's never been done before. If this is the case, it's to be hoped you find an agent who shares your vision, because your book could become a genre-busting sensation that has a lasting influence on the literary canon ...

3.  ... but the other way to look at it is that there could be good reasons for why nobody has published a book like this before. Is it something that people are actually going to want to buy?

## How do I know if an agent is looking for new authors?

Check the submissions guidelines page of their agency website and follow them on social media. Most agents – even those with a large list – remain open to receiving submissions, often out of a fear of missing out on a book they'd love to work on.

If an agent moves agencies, is leaving the industry altogether, takes a sabbatical or feels they are working at capacity, they should update their agency bio to say they are no longer accepting submissions.

## Is it possible to meet agents prior to submitting?

It's now fairly commonplace for agents to speak at writing events, of which there has been an explosion across the UK. Whether at one of the established book fairs or literary festivals, a publisher-backed conference or a smaller event run by an independent bookstore, agents are often in demand as speakers because writers want to hear about what they want and ask them questions. Every single *Writers & Artists* event held over the past ten years has had attendees ask questions about the submission process.

As above, and as has become second nature to a lot of writers, social media can also be a great tool for 'getting to know' an agent. Watching or listening to interviews is another good way to get an idea of what type of writing appeals to agents, while there are dozens of written interviews available to read on writersandartists.co.uk, too.

# Is attending book fairs a good way to get an agent?

No. Even though over recent years book fairs have become more accessible to unpublished writers (encouraged by being able to see what's going on via websites and social media buzz from authors/agents/editors), with the most established fairs taking place in London (March/April), Bologna (March/April) and Frankfurt (October), usually over four-day periods.

If you're an unrepresented writer paying to attend, there'll be a reasonable amount taking place that will be of interest (author talks, for example), but it's important to manage your expectations: paying an entrance fee to a book fair does *not* mean it is your big chance to pitch your book to an agent. The more likely scenario is you'll be given short shrift and encouraged to visit their agency website to follow their submission guidelines.

Why? Because major book fairs are key industry events and agents need to do a great deal of preparation to be ready for them. They set up meetings with editors from international publishers and try to sell the rights of their existing clients' books. A lot of effort goes into these meetings (with authors pushed hard to ensure their manuscript is honed and ready to go should there be interest); as a result, new authors seeking representation cannot be agents' main concern at that time. It's best for you to wait a couple of weeks and be safe in the knowledge that you're not sending your book off to someone exhausted from a book fair, but rather to an agent who's had time to get their energy back before continuing their search for new writing talent.

# How long does it take to get an agent?

There really is no straightforward answer to this. If you have a great manuscript, you've researched the agents you're going to submit to, and there's a case of 'right place, right time', then an offer of representation could come within a day or two.

This is a dream scenario, though. What's more likely, due to the sheer volume of submissions an agent receives and the relatively small amount of time they have each day to actually read them, is that you have to expect to wait a couple of months before hearing back. Most agency websites state a response time of between eight and twelve weeks, so let your expectations be guided by that estimate.

If an agent is impressed by what they've read in your submission, they will then make contact to ask to read the full manuscript. At this stage, the response time is likely to be much shorter. If they decide against offering representation, it's likely they will provide feedback. If they remain interested, a call – or, ideally, a meeting – will be arranged to discuss things further. This meeting could culminate in an offer of representation, perhaps after a cooling-off period of a couple of days.

SEE ALSO *How do I know when to stop editing?* on page 52 and *Dealing with rejection and starting over* page 174.

## Can I be represented by an agent if I'm under eighteen?

This is possible, it's just a situation that doesn't occur that often. A client under the age of eighteen might decide against mentioning their age in their covering letter or even after receiving a full-read request, but if an agent gets in touch to arrange a call or meeting to discuss the manuscript further, it's advisable to make them aware. It shouldn't be a problem per se, it's just making sure the central focus of any meeting is your manuscript (and not surprise at how young you are). Also, an agent might prefer a parent or guardian to be present at the meeting, and if a representation agreement is offered, then they might ask their agency to provide a short-term one for a parent to sign.

## Will an agent want to represent me if I'm an older writer?

It's all about the book, so this shouldn't be an issue. Yes, agents and publishing houses do love younger writers because they come with the excitement of what's to come ... but an agent (or publisher) is still unlikely to turn down a well-crafted book they believe will sell just because the author is seventy. Age, and anything else for that matter, should always be secondary to their opinion of the writing. Also, who's to say a 70-year-old writer won't have books number two, three and four tucked away in a bottom drawer and, editorial fine-tuning aside, ready to go? Meanwhile, the 21-year-old writing sensation could be lost amidst the pressures of writing a second book and stall in delivering to their publisher.

## Should I pay an agent to represent me?

No. An agent gets paid only from charging commission on royalties earned by their authors. As noted previously, all reputable agents operate in this way, complying with the Association of Authors' Agents (AAA) code of practice, which is free to view in full online (www.agentsassoc. co.uk/about/code-of-practice/). Not one penny should be earned by an agent in relation to your work until you earn money too: no reading fees, no money for editorial guidance, nothing. When they offer to represent you, an agent is fully aware that all editorial feedback, career guidance and approach of commissioning editors with your work are services that stand to go unpaid until the rights to your book are sold to a publisher and they pay the first instalment of the advance on royalties they offer you. As a partnership, therefore, your interests are entirely aligned: to get your book published.

The offer of an advance on royalties is agreed as part of a publishing agreement to acquire the rights to an author's manuscript. It tends to be broken up into three instalments (on signature, manuscript delivery, and on publication), with each instalment transferred by the publisher to your agent's agency account. At this point, your agent will take their agreed commission on this figure (15 per cent for a UK deal, as already outlined), then transfer the rest to you. This is the first money your book generates for you, and therefore the first time your agent will receive money for their work in representing you.

And the advance on royalties will remain the only money either the writer or agent receive from this particular deal (an agent will try to sell rights to publishers operating in other territories, as well as film, TV and audio rights, meaning other agreements linked to the same book could generate further royalties) until enough copies have been sold to surpass the advance on royalties already paid out by the publisher. However, once the author's share of the sales exceed the value of that figure, the writer will begin accruing royalties. Their agent, therefore, will then continue to charge commission at the agreed rate of 15 per cent.

SEE ALSO *What's an author advance?* page 213.

## How many debut writers does an agent take on each year?

Relative to the number of submissions an agent receives …? Not many.

An agent with a healthy list of published clients, for example, will always keep an eye on the submissions coming through just in case something comes in that really grabs them. Realistically, though, they probably don't have the bandwidth to add more than one or two unpublished writers to their books, particularly those they think will need a lot of their time editorially. If you write fiction, this is why it's imperative not to put your manuscript out on submission until it's both finished and as good as you can make it. If the odds are against you already, at least make sure your manuscript leaves an agent with a tough decision to make.

Some agents, however, might keep their list of clients small deliberately, preferring to work closely with each writer while also keeping their workload in check. Agents new to the game might be actively looking to grow their list, and could take on three, four, five or more authors within a calendar year. With fewer published clients to manage deals for and therefore more of their time available in comparison, could an agent at this stage of their career be one to target ahead of agents who represent big-name authors?

# PART II

*The submission process*

# Is my manuscript ready?

Before starting to send your manuscript out to agents, ask yourself a brutal but necessary question: is my manuscript ready? You are the only one who will know when it is.

After all of the time and effort you've put into producing a 'finished' version of your manuscript, one thing you owe your writing is honesty. There's no definite way to know what's 'ready', and no agent is expecting your manuscript to land in their inbox in an immediately publishable state. Every piece of writing can be improved, and it's part of an agent's job to develop their authors' manuscript, asking questions of plot and character and suggesting different ways to piece things together. True, they're looking for a strong authorial voice, a consistent quality of writing that leads a reader from page to page, and ideas and/or characters that grab them; all of which is no mean feat. But they're not necessarily looking for perfection.

So, what does 'Is my manuscript ready?' mean, then? For our purposes, it actually means 'is my manuscript *submission*-ready?' Do you think you've reached a point of not being able to develop your manuscript any further, that you've produced a piece of writing you're happy to put in front of an industry professional? If you're writing fiction, a good way to gauge this is to ask yourself the following:

- have you finished it?
- have you taken a break from it?
- has it been re-written *at least* once?
- do you think it's appropriate for your target audience?
- has someone other than your best friend read it ...?
- ... and have you actually listened to their feedback?
- have you rewritten it again?

And perhaps most importantly:

- is it honestly as good as you can possibly make it?

Any agent you submit to will expect you to be able to answer 'Yes' to all of the above because they're tried and trusted steps to making sure a manuscript is in a reasonable shape. Stress-testing your work in such a way (and developing your manuscript based on the different feedback you'll have received as a result) has the added benefit of strengthening your resolve as an author. Taking this sort of approach means you've moved way beyond being that writer excited by an idea who then sends out a first draft 'to see if anyone thinks it's any good'. Instead, you're taking a more professional approach; one that's going to leave your manuscript in a better shape. (Take a look back at your first draft and see what you think.) The chances of your submission staying in the game are likely to have improved by doing so.

## How do I know when to stop editing?

This is a tricky one for you to answer, especially if you're a perfectionist by nature. Writers can have a tendency to get too close to their book, obsessing over individual sentences but remaining blind to wider structural issues. And this endless tinkering can also cause a project to become too dense and over-engineered. Perhaps heeding the advice of many an agent and getting to the end before stepping away from your manuscript for (at least) a couple of weeks could be the way to go? A new perspective comes from returning to a book with fresh eyes, and it's a simple technique anyone can apply to help unmask flaws. Are there sections where the writing is really good but other parts where it's quite flat? Are there easy typos you can fix? These are all things to sort out ahead of an agent reading through your work.

This points us towards an absolute golden rule of the submission process: never even contemplate sending out a first draft. Or if you do, know that no justifiable argument can be made for your manuscript *actually* being ready. The first draft is about you getting to know your narrative, meaning there are definitely areas that could be improved. An agent doesn't want to see this version. They're working on the basis that the minimum expectation an author has in submitting their work is that they take it seriously. They therefore assume the version of the manuscript they're reading is one that's the result of the author pushing themselves to capacity. Which is not to say they're looking for perfection, just definitely not a file containing some of the very-fixable flaws of which first drafts are often guilty. Allow yourself the chance to tighten dialogue, improve descriptions and interrogate how the whole thing hangs together.

Another way to understand the parts of your book that work (or not) is to get feedback from readers. Are there people you know that you can trust to give you firm but fair thoughts? Were there plot points they didn't quite follow? How did they feel towards your main character? Being able to listen to constructive criticism is essential, and these sorts of considerations could prove invaluable ahead of submitting to an industry professional.

And you are going to have to do this, eventually. After re-drafting, taking time away and taking on board the comments of beta readers (people who read an early draft of an author's manuscript and offers their thoughts on it), you've done as much as you can for the good of your manuscript. So even if *you* think there are still areas that aren't quite right, as long as your readers haven't found these sections to be an issue, it's time to take the plunge.

## Will an agent take on a manuscript that needs work?

If there's something there, either in the narrative voice or the way the concept of a manuscript is introduced, then an agent could still offer representation to a manuscript that needs a fair bit of work. Structural issues can be fixed, but the way every author tells a story is different, and if this is the bit that's unique and excites an agent, it might be enough to make them want to at least encourage you to stay in touch and re-submit in a few months' time.

You can't expect every agent to do this, though, because taking on a new manuscript is a gamble; an investment of their time and expertise that might never pay dividends. The very fact that agents don't receive any money in relation to their clients' work until a publisher has bought the rights to their manuscript means, out of necessity, they will exercise a degree of caution towards the writers they decide to commit their time to. Submitting an unpolished manuscript obviously lowers the chances of your work being prioritised over that of another writer in their Submissions folder. Basically, there's a big difference between a manuscript that needs a bit of guidance to help it flourish, and one that shows flashes of talent but reeks of a lack of care and attention. And agents, who receive at least fifty submissions each week, can spot an 'Oh, this will do' attitude from a mile away.

## Should I show people my book before I submit?

If you're going to be a professional author, then that means letting other people read your work. The question is, do you really want the first person to read your manuscript to be a literary agent?

A more prudent approach might be to source some feedback from other people first, as mentioned above. But which people do you know who meet the criteria of being big readers (ideally readers of the genre you're writing in), and someone you can trust to provide honest feedback on *both* the pros and cons of your manuscript?

*Friends/Family*: it's more than reasonable to ask friends/family for their thoughts on your work (not least because the writing of it could well have impacted on your relationship with them!) but before you do ask yourself: *Are they going to be honest enough? Are you going to get the bad stuff as well as the good?* This is because an *objective* critical appraisal is going to help you develop your writing much more than your mum saying 'It's brilliant – I'm so proud of you'. Who have you spoken to about your writing before? What about a colleague? Don't just revert to your nearest and dearest because it's an easy option.

*Online forums:* are you a member of an online writing forum? If so, have you contributed small pieces of writing and therefore feel confident in contacting a group of people who have critiqued your work in the past? Twitter can also be a good place for striking up a writing relationship with people genuinely interested in the same sort of books as you. Perhaps you follow someone who blogs book reviews? Maybe you follow an editor who regularly tweets editing tips or writing advice? Users of social media do tend to have an idea of people who have interacted with their posts over a period of time so it's not too much of a leap of faith that they'd be willing to offer some thoughts on your work.

*Local reading/Writing groups:* these can be hard to come by but if you don't feel comfortable talking to friends or family about your writing, try your local library, book shop or cafe to see if there's a local writing group or book club that meets up regularly. This could at least open up the possibility of finding one or two people interested in writing who, after a while, you might want to share your work with.

Perhaps most important of all when identifying potential beta readers, however, is how confident you are in their approach to the concept of offering feedback. Every writer is vulnerable when someone reads their work for the first time, and this will be especially true if you've never shared your writing before. Your audience showing a bit of empathy with what you're trying to achieve and also being constructive in their criticism therefore becomes key to you retaining confidence. This doesn't mean that you should only ask those people who'll be nice to you, but that you should think about who you can trust to be honest, and who will offer reasons behind their thinking on what, in their opinion, does and doesn't work. Why do they dislike a character? Why didn't they understand what was happening? It doesn't matter whether you entirely agree with the points they make so long as they come with an explanation.

SEE ALSO *What if I don't agree with the editorial changes suggested by my agent?* page 201.

## Should I pay an editor to look at my work?

Paid-for editorial services are a good option for writers who feel their manuscript needs professional guidance to make progress. They can, however, come at a significant cost and in no way should be considered essential to a book reaching a publishable standard. Agents are not expecting to receive a submission that's been looked at by anyone beyond beta readers sourced by the writer.

As with any expensive product, doing some research before buying is sensible. There are a host of organisations that link writers to freelance editors, with writersandartists.co.uk an obvious provider of services for different stages of the writing and editing process. It's wise to assess all options, though, first to compare prices but also as a catalyst for thinking more deeply about what you stand to get for your investment. Is it a line-by-line copy-edit or a read and review report that would benefit your work the most at this stage? And what experience does the editor have? Do they come recommended, either from a writer you know or through testimonials from other authors? And finally, are you comfortable with having to absorb the cost of employing them to work on your manuscript despite zero guarantee that you will go on to be published?

# Do I need to finish my manuscript before submitting?

There are always exceptions to the rule but, depending on the type of book you're writing, here are the basic guidelines:

FICTION

The safe answer here is yes. There will always be a recent exception of a bewitching first three chapters and knockout story concept being enough to secure representation, but it's more realistic to prepare for the fact you're going to need to have a full manuscript ready to read before an agent wants to take you on. This is for two reasons:

1. writing the ending of a book often completely changes your thinking about the best way to deliver your beginning. Until you can step back and look at the book in its entirety, it's impossible to be absolutely sure that things tie up in the way you'd originally planned – nor can you be sure your opening section is quite as impactful as it should be. To pitch an as-yet unfinished book to an agent is to pitch something you're not really sure fits together in the best way possible. And remember, you're also required to provide an agent with a synopsis for the book as a whole;

2. imagine an agent reads your first three chapters and is so enthralled that they push everything else to one side. They then call/email and ask to read your work in full:

   'I need to know what happens next,' says the agent.

   'That's great,' you reply, 'but you're going to have to wait six months because I'd planned to finish it when I go travelling around south-east Asia.'

   'Oh,' says the agent. 'Well, send it again when you're done.'

And while it *could* all be fine (you've done enough to grab attention in the first place, and the agent may be willing to wait as a result), an agent might be too busy or have lost interest by the time they finally read the rest of your book. Why take such an unnecessary gamble with the fate of your book and career as an author? Yes, talent will always have a chance of coming through, but serendipity seems to have a hand in things too. In such a subjective, taste and zeitgeist-driven industry can you guarantee you'll get another chance? In making an agent wait, no matter how good the remainder of the manuscript turns out to be when they finally get their hands on it, you have to accept it's not going to provide the same thrill as when they first stopped everything to contact you, desperate to read beyond those opening chapters.

### NON-FICTION

Pitching without a completed manuscript is more acceptable in narrative-led popular non-fiction (and definitely so in the case of any non-narrative non-fiction, whether this be for the popular or academic market). This is because non-fiction projects can depend on factors beyond the author, such as a photographer, a research trip or to coincide with capturing a particular event: funding for which may need to come from the publisher. As part of a non-fiction proposal, most agents ask for a covering letter that introduces the project (Why this book? Why now? Why this author?), a chapter breakdown and at least one sample chapter. The chapter summary is expected to be a more extensive document than a fiction synopsis, providing a breakdown of what the author is set to cover within each section and the overall shape the book is set to take, while the writing sample is obviously a means to provide an idea of the quality of the prose the author is going to produce.

Memoir, however, is the exception to the rule here. Although technically non-fiction, memoirs (and some biography titles too) tend to be dealt with in the same manner as fiction in that they require conventional narrative structures and an engaging authorial voice to keep readers turning pages. As a result, an agent will need to see, and probably need to work on editorially, the entire manuscript before sending it out to prospective publishers (although there's a more relaxed stance on this with celebrity authors, who can secure book deals way ahead of a manuscript being finished purely because publishers hope that public interest in their back story will lead to strong book sales).

## What's an average word count for the type of book I'm writing?

There will always be a book you can point to that flies in the face of the figures below, but here are some general average word-count expectations per book type:

*General adult fiction:* this refers to commercial, from crime and thriller through to romance. Word counts considered to be the norm are anything between 80,000 and 100,000 words. Exceeding 100,000 words might mean questions around exposition and pacing, while falling way below 80,000 might lead to concerns about a story being under-developed.

*Genre fiction:* there's an understanding that sci-fi, fantasy or historical fiction may need to be longer (120,000 words or more) because building the world (the landscape and/or the internal logic) is intrinsic to the concept of the book. For established authors with a solid fanbase in these genres (particularly authors of series), maximum word counts tend not to matter provided readers continue to buy new releases. An author like George R. R. Martin, whose books can come in at more than 250,000 words, is a good example. Consider this before trying to pitch a debut novel of a similar length.

*Literary fiction:* as noted above the Venn diagram of what's commercial and what's literary is something to be argued over forever. And unfortunately, so can the typical word count of a piece of literary fiction. Some have weighed in around the novella-length of 60,000 words, but readers of this genre also wouldn't baulk at a debut touching 120,000 words.

*Young adult (YA) fiction:* aimed at readers aged thirteen and above, a debut book would have a lower-end word count of approximately 60,000 words, while a maximum would be in the region of 80,000.

*Middle-grade fiction:* it's worth constantly reading up on reader trends and expectations because both could have an influence on what's now considered to be an acceptable word count, particularly in this ever-evolving category of books. Lower middle-grade books are those written for readers aged between seven and nine, while upper middle-grade books (being careful not to stray into the more adult themes tackled in YA fiction) tend to be for 9–12 year-olds. If you're writing for younger readers, then anything between 25,000 and 45,000 words is permissible (illustrations can have an impact on word length), while up to 60,000 words is about right for the older tier.

*Picture books:* these could have fewer than 100 words but get nowhere near 1,000.

*Non-narrative non-fiction:* expectations obviously vary according to your audience. The in-depth nature of academic or specialist texts can lead to them being at least 80,000 words but again, the word count should always correspond with whether the subject matter has been dealt with in sufficient detail. Heavily illustrated titles tend to have a lower word counts.

*Narrative non-fiction:* like a standard work of fiction, an autobiography or memoir is likely to be in the 80- to 100,000-word bracket.

If you find yourself drastically outside of the relevant word count guidelines suggested above, it might be worth considering whether your narrative is developed enough, or you need to spend some time tightening how your story unfolds. That said, if you're confident you know your market and you're convinced the length of your manuscript feels right for the story you're trying to tell (and you've had feedback from beta readers to say as much), then by all means stick to your guns. A prospective agent is likely to put questions your way regarding structure, scene length and character development anyway, so this sort of discussion might lead to the length of your manuscript changing anyway.

# Submitting a manuscript: preparing your documents

One of the most difficult things for a writer to come to terms with after many months (sometimes years) of living inside the creative bubble of actually finishing a manuscript is to suddenly change tack and conform to 'business mode'. Yet that's precisely what's required in putting together a manuscript submission. Adhering to agency guidelines is all part of this, and doing so means your book stands a better chance of being accepted. Keep the following basic principles in mind.

- Once a manuscript is acquired it receives an edit, a cover, a sale price and a marketing campaign. In short, it becomes a real book, and books are *products* which publishers have invested in and want to profit from. Always try to stay true to your writing but do understand that in trying to become published what you've produced is no longer *just* for you: a company deciding to invest in your writing means they want it to have an appeal among a target audience, and your agent and publishing house team will base decisions around this.

- It can help to think about trying to get an agent as being like trying to get a job. Yes, it can be frustrating and time-consuming to prepare the relevant documents, but it's necessary to do so if you're going to be considered for the role. Sending your manuscript to an agent isn't quite the same as applying to become a worker bee for a huge conglomerate, though. You're trying to find a creative ally. Someone with whom you'll have close-knit discussions about the direction of your writing; who you'll trust to raise awareness of your manuscript and then do their best to have a publisher buy it.

- Agents have particular submission guidelines and request certain documents for two reasons: first, it allows them to quickly process the huge number of manuscripts they receive; second, it provides the fairest way to get a sense of whether the writing is for them, and also an idea of what the author might be like to work with.

In short, submission guidelines are part of the process; do you and your manuscript justice by following them. They're *not* there just to make you jump through hoops, but rather for the practical purposes of ensuring that agents can process submissions in a manner that allows them to concentrate solely on the standard of the writing. Why wouldn't you take the opportunity to put the agent you're submitting to in a positive frame of mind before they've even read the first sentence of your manuscript?

## What should a manuscript submission consist of?

Always check the submission guidelines of each individual agent you're querying and ensure you follow them carefully. The following are generalities only.

- *Fiction:* one-page covering letter, one-page synopsis, opening three chapters or first 10,000 words.
- *Middle grade/YA:* as above.
- *Picturebooks:* one-page covering letter, short synopsis, full text of single picturebook. A page-spread that corresponds with the picturebook text may be asked for if available.
- *Non-fiction (narrative, such as autobiography/memoir):* one-page covering letter, one-page synopsis, opening three chapters or first 10,000 words.

- *Non-fiction (non-narrative):* one-page covering letter, five-page chapter outline, sample of writing (can range from just the first chapter to the first three).

## What are the main differences between submitting fiction and non-fiction?

On the face of it there doesn't appear to be a great deal between the documents expected within a fiction and non-fiction proposal. There are subtle differences, though, and failing to acknowledge their importance may undermine the chances of your project.

Where fiction is concerned, it's all about the manuscript. Is the writing to a high standard, is the concept for the book an intriguing one, does it fit nicely within the marketplace, and is there something about the narrative voice that takes the book to a level above the other submissions an agent is reading within that genre? The covering letter and synopsis are necessary additions to the manuscript and should be treated with care but, unless either is off-puttingly bad, it's the power of a book's opening that will lead to an agent showing an interest and requesting to read the full manuscript.

Narrative non-fiction projects require a covering letter, chapter breakdown and a writing sample. Within the covering letter, though, the credentials of the author are considered much more closely. Whereas fiction proposals are all about the writing, prose and narrative structure, non-fiction proposals must be accompanied by the not insignificant extras of author authenticity, topical interest and, within the memoir/biography genre, a relatability that will encourage readers to invest in a uniquely personal account. Agents understand that publishers choose to buy this type of book based on these elements, and this can lead to much frustration among writers of memoir and biography who fail to get a publishing deal. What can you do if someone doesn't deem your personal story to be one that's remarkable enough to strike a chord with a wider audience?

Finally, a word on the difference in focus given to the documents a writer needs to provide when pitching a non-narrative non-fiction book to an agent. A covering letter is required and will need to contain sufficient detail about the concept of the book, its author and its intended audience. Then come three important Whys: Why is this author the right person to write the book? Why is this book different to those already published on the same subject? And why is *now* the right time to publish the book? Compelling answers to these questions will convince an agent to believe in the book, and hopefully a commissioning editor, too. A well-planned chapter breakdown is also needed, though, and this is a document an agent and author will work on extensively ahead of the proposal going out on submission to prospective editors. How does the author intend to cover the subject matter in a way that keeps the reader invested? Like the synopsis for a work of fiction, the chapter outline is expected to be a roadmap of the manuscript. It can, however, be more detailed: key points of learning (as well as headline statistics or quotes if they're essential to a section) should definitely appear.

Put simply, the reason the chapter breakdown holds such significance to an agent is because, provided the writing sample is of reasonable quality, the prose doesn't actually become a primary concern until a publisher acquires the rights to the project.

## Some agents ask for a 'writing CV'. Do I need one?

It isn't that common for 'writing experience' to be asked for in a separate document as most agents expect anything like this just to be included in your covering letter. If a CV document is asked for, though, it's likely for there to be some explanatory text on the agency website to give you a steer on what might be included (being placed in a recognised competition, award nominations, courses you've completed, other books published, etc.). It's also unlikely for this document to be one that's mandatory. Writers aren't expected, for example, to hold a Creative

Writing MA or to have won a short story award. It's great to have done so, of course, but if you've simply written a book in your spare time every morning before work then that doesn't make your submission any less relevant or exciting.

## What's the purpose of the submission package?

It enables agents to receive submissions in a form that they find quickest and easiest to process, while also providing those that submit with the opportunity to write a personal approach that introduces what their book is about, who they think it's for, and why they think the recipient would like it.

A lot of writers, however, find it frustrating that there isn't a standardised way to submit to multiple agents at once. This is understandable, as preparing individual submissions can be a lengthy process. Yet the reason standardisation can't really be brought in is because every agent has a slightly different way of working (personal preferences, agency website functionality, submissions across different types of books), and this has to be prioritised given the huge number of submissions they receive each week. As already mentioned, the reading of these is often done outside of general working hours (which need to be dedicated to authors they already represent) so agents have to quickly sort everything as efficiently as possible. Every writer submitting to one particular agent will need to abide by the same guidelines, providing a level playing field for every writer hoping to gain representation.

It's also worth reiterating that agents *want* you to have done a bit of research on them before submitting your manuscript. If you're serious about asking them to represent you and your work (and have them charge commission on your royalties for the privilege), this seems a reasonable assumption to make. And those authors who haven't complied with submission guidelines will be quickly spotted by the agents and weeded out.

## How many submissions does an agent receive each year?

It's impossible to provide an accurate figure but for context of the amount of competition you face as well as how much unsolicited submissions occupy an agent's time, a general average to work with is for an agent to receive between fifty and 100 per week. And this is a fairly conservative estimate; agents who work at well-known agencies and/or represent bestselling authors can receive well over double this amount. Agents at boutique agencies, however, may not receive quite so many, particularly during the quieter summer months.

## How do I make my proposal stand out from the crowd?

There really is no 'cheat' to your work getting ahead. Agents are simply looking for something within their area of interest, and then that golden combination of brilliant concept plus high-quality writing. And as their search is only really focused on finding this, they are very much against gimmicks – a tactic some writers (albeit innocently a lot of the time) employ to try and give their book an edge.

Gimmicks, such as quirky fonts, links to videos, pages of illustrations or any other factor that's in some way associated to the manuscript, will only ever succeed in diluting an agent's attention towards the writing itself. This is a false move on the part of the writer, because the writing is the only thing that will convince an agent to make an offer of representation.

Finally, gimmicks also include door-stepping of any kind, which is an absolute no-no. Showing up in the reception area of an agency with a manuscript gift-wrapped alongside a box of chocolates, thrusting a copy into an agent's hands at an event, or making follow-up phone calls within just a few days of submitting will all end up deflecting attention away from (rather than drawing it toward) your manuscript.

# Do agents read everything they get sent?

It might take a while for them to get to your submission but agents at least *look* at everything they've been sent. And with gusto – but *only* up until they see it's not for them. So your job as the writer is two-fold: to make sure you're submitting something within the bounds of what an agent represents; and to make sure your writing is so good that it makes it difficult for them to say no to offering representation.

How you present yourself within your submission in general obviously plays a part in this. It's the first impression you make upon them as a writer, after all. What chance are you giving yourself, for example, if your submission to an agent based at a medium or large agency leads with a poorly written covering letter addressed to no one in particular and that details a book for 5–8 year-olds when not a single person at the agency represents children's fiction? In this case, quite rightly, you can't expect an agent to give your work anything other than a cursory glance.

To take this example one step further, larger agencies that receive huge numbers of submissions may employ agency readers or provide senior agents with an assistant. These roles can act as an initial filter for opening and sorting unsolicited submissions, immediately screening established agents from submissions that are clearly a waste of their time (while submissions that show promise are sent on to the relevant agent for consideration). This isn't all that common, however, as most agencies have neither the desire nor the means to employ assistants or readers. Pretty much all agents accept (and enjoy!) the responsibility of reading unsolicited submissions, provided they are of good quality and within the bounds of the types of books they represent. They therefore approach this protracted task positively, enthusiastic in the hope of unearthing a book they fall in love with.

As mentioned earlier, agents have so many demands on their time within office hours that they often read manuscripts outside of work: on the commute, over lunch, or in a cafe at the weekend. It's through no fault of your own that you're encroaching on an agent's spare time but help where you can by giving them as little to do as possible. They want a succinct and professional covering letter, and for documents attached to adhere to their submission guidelines. This is immediately going to make them warm to you, and, most importantly, it's going to mean the sole focus of their concentration is the opening chapters of your manuscript. Whether they go on to offer representation or not, approaching the submission process in this way means you've done all you can; you've done the very best by your writing, and this professional approach won't be lost on any other agent you query.

## Do I submit by email or by post?

As you might expect, the vast majority of agency websites ask for e-submissions. Don't take this for granted, though, so check all agency guidelines before preparing your submission. As stated at the beginning of this section, the primary reason for these guidelines is to assist agents in processing and assessing submissions in a way that suits them (and not to make it as awkward as possible for the writer). An agent might not want an e-submission to come with more than one attachment, for example, and to be in a certain file type because they read all unsolicited manuscripts on a particular device. (If you send three or four files, and in the wrong format, the agent *might* bother to paste it all together and convert them. Or they might give up and turn to another submission instead.)

Finally, if you send in a submission by post then there's even more reason to check the guidelines stated on the website. Does it need to be sent via recorded delivery? Will your manuscript be returned to you if you enclose a stamped, self-addressed envelope?

# Should I submit everything as separate documents?

Again, check agency guidelines carefully. You may be asked to split some documents and/or combine others.

If you're submitting a work of adult, middle-grade or YA fiction, or you've written a memoir or autobiography, it's likely you'll be asked to submit the following by email: covering letter, synopsis, and either the opening three chapters or the first 10,000 words of your manuscript. Usually the expectation is for your covering letter to be in the body of your email, and the other two documents attached (meaning each chapter should not be a separate file). If you really feel there's a need to submit something extra – such as a map of the world in which your fantasy novel is set, or a photo referenced at the beginning of a memoir – then perhaps go with your gut, but in the knowledge it must be *absolutely essential* to include. If not, perhaps mention it in your covering letter as being available upon request. This leaves the agent to judge your writing on its own merits, aware that there's more material to come besides the manuscript if they want it.

If you're submitting a picture book for children, you're likely to be asked for a covering letter which contains the synopsis of the book. The expectation is that this should come alongside the full manuscript. You may also be encouraged to attach a page-spread that correlates with the text. A page-spread is a helicopter-view document used to illustrate how the author thinks the manuscript will flow, with particular focus given to the placing of sentences and artwork on the page. This is because page-turns play a key part in the rhythm (and humour) of a picture book. So yes, if you have produced artwork relating to your picture-book text, it *could* be included here. It's important to stress, however, that for some agents this runs the risk of you being overly prescriptive. In submitting to a literary agent you're putting yourself forward as a writer, not an illustrator. If an offer of representation and a publishing contract come your way, your agent knows the editor at your publisher will have their own ideas about illustrators they'd like to commission to work on your book, and that they'll expect creative freedom.

Writers of non-narrative popular non-fiction will be asked for a covering letter and a writing sample but may be expected to provide a much fuller outline of the book. Rather than a synopsis this is known as a 'chapter outline': it needs to be a more detailed document due to there being an understanding the manuscript won't be finished (or even started) until the project has been commissioned by the publisher.

SEE ALSO *I've written a children's picture book. Can I submit artwork too?* page 72.

## Are email subject lines important?

As long as it represents what the email contains then, in relation to the quality of your writing and concept of your book, your subject line isn't all that important.

To look at it another way, though, a subject line could definitely qualify as one of those minor, intangible dud notes that lead an agent to conclude your submission doesn't quite meet the standard or style of work they're looking to represent. You have to assume the standard of the other writers submitting to the same agent is very high, so if getting the little details right means your approach creates that little bit more of a positive impression then consider it time well spent. And after all, your subject line is the very first thing about your book that an agent sees. A typo isn't a great start, then.

In general, you can expect any specifics within submission guidelines to amount to requests that they begin with words like 'SUBMISSION:' or 'FAO Agent Name'. (Again, this probably comes back to the organisational methods of an agent in order to deal with a lot of incoming submissions.) Otherwise, it's reasonable to expect an agent with an individual submissions email address will want a subject line simply to state 'Book Title by Author Name'. And if you find your submission needs to be sent to a generic submissions@ email address, agency guidelines may tell you how to make it clear within the subject line that you'd like your material to be read by a particular agent: 'Book Title by Author Name (FAO Agent Name).'

## How important are grammar, spelling and punctuation?

By sending a book proposal to a literary agent you're asking an industry professional to spend time assessing your writing and, ultimately, consider whether it can reach a publishable standard. The documents included within your submission therefore need to do the job of creating a good first impression and in publishing, perhaps more than any other industry, it's mandatory for grammar, spelling and punctuation to be of a high standard.

Agents genuinely accept that mistakes happen, though, so if one has crept into your documents and you've not realised before clicking 'Send', then it's not a cause for panic. Yes, it's annoying for you, but it's more annoying for the agent if you start sending follow up emails to explain, or call their office in a flap to find out whether or not they've opened your submission in the hope you can resend. Trust in the fact that your mistake will be put in context with the overall quality of your submission. If this is to a high standard, it would be churlish for an agent to disregard your entire book because you used 'there' instead of 'their'.

If mistakes are the norm rather than the exception, however, your chances of being offered representation will fall. For typos to appear regularly is quite damning given the free spell-check tools widely available. Could they be simply down to laziness on your part? Dyslexic authors may find spelling a genuine challenge (and this is something to be upfront about in your covering letter) but still get published because they work hard to correct mistakes and use beta readers to help them identify errors before approaching agents with their manuscript.

Ultimately, ask yourself this: if you haven't paid the correct amount of attention to your work then why should an agent (especially when there can be no certainty the book will go on to be acquired and published)? If you have an absolutely stellar idea for a book that really captures the imagination of an agent who is just starting out and hungry to grow their list then, yes, *maybe* there's a chance they'll commit an inordinate amount of time to ironing out your mistakes, but rest assured they'd rather sign up authors who push themselves to produce work that reaches as high a standard as possible.

## I've written a children's picture book. Can I submit artwork too?

Unless submission guidelines state otherwise, if you're the *writer* of a children's picture book then your expectation should be to submit the text alone. If you submit a page-spread document to give an idea of the rhythm of the book, the inclusion of any artwork could lead to you running the risk of appearing inflexible with regard to how you'd like your book illustrated. Would you be difficult to work with as a result? Are your expecting to be able to contribute your own illustrations? At this stage of your career, if you're approaching an agent as an author then it's best to make sure this remains their focus.

If you class yourself as a picture book *illustrator,* then you need to state as much in your covering letter, which should also provide links to a website showcasing more of your work. It's not uncommon for children's book agents to represent writers and illustrators but more unusual to find agents that represent author-illustrators. To be an *author-illustrator* you have to excel in both fields. Even if you're a very competent illustrator, until you become a recognised name within the picture books field (i.e. books are sold under your name), it's unlikely a publisher will go with your illustrations when they have contacts for the best in the business. A 'known' illustrator's name appearing against your story for example, gives it a greater chance of selling and the publisher a better chance of seeing a return on the investment they have made in the product. Once established (in the sense that parents will be looking out for more of your books), there's every chance you could negotiate illustrating your own stories.

## How do I protect my work throughout the submission process?

If you're nervous about someone lifting sections of your text or stealing your idea, remember that UK copyright law works to protect you provided you're able to prove your manuscript is your intellectual property. This can be done by simply being able to provide versions of how the manuscript has progressed, while email timestamps automatically generated by, for example, submitting your work to agents are further proof. If you are nervous about submitting something by post, then organise a recorded delivery to ensure proof of the manuscript being sent out by you, and that it has been received.

On a more general note, when submitting to an agent it's probably wise to tone down any concerns you might harbour about your work/ idea being pinched. Part of the process of working with an agent is that you're willing to place trust in them, from editorial advice through to negotiating the sale of rights to your work. Although the *Writers' & Artists' Yearbook* is a large book and search engine results for prospective appropriate agents might appear endless, as soon as you start doing serious research into who might actually be interested in your manuscript then your corner of the publishing industry quickly reduces in size. It really does make no business sense, therefore, for an agent to risk their reputation by getting involved with something as murky as giving your story to one of their established writers and asking them to go away and write their version. Even in the (highly unlikely) case that the worst did happen, publishing is just too small a world for those responsible not to be found out.

# Submitting a manuscript: your approach to submitting

Not only does the whole submission process bring a modicum of order to the large number of new books being pitched to agents, it benefits writers too, in that it creates a level playing field for all. More or less every writer gets to submit the same amount of writing and, provided agency guidelines are followed and the manuscript is directed towards those agents most likely to be interested in representing the book, everyone's submission will get read.

Some more home truths, though. The process of submitting your work to various agents may prove to be a frustrating one, especially if rejection letters begin to pile up. It's therefore important to make sure you're approaching things in the right way: that you have a plan, your expectations are in check, and that all of this doesn't bring about a creative rut. Which agents are you going to approach? How are you going to organise yourself in sending out submissions? Do you know what the expected response time is of each agent you're submitting to? Have you taken a break from your manuscript? Have you actually considered that bit of feedback you received from readers even though it's a change you might find painful to make? Also, as you prepare to go into new territory with your current manuscript and get into the groove of submitting to agents, is there anything else you could begin working on? Could you be researching, or plotting chapter summaries ahead of your next book?

Here are some final things to consider before you get into the practicalities of sitting down to present your work to agents.

# Do I need to finish my book before submitting to agents?

FICTION

An agent's job is to sell the rights to a *complete* story, not just the beginning of one. How can you submit a work of fiction in the knowledge that every scene unfolds with as great an impact as it should if you haven't yet written the ending?

While stories with a great hook and startling beginning are always going to make an agent sit up and pay attention, ultimately they're looking for a well-developed book. A reminder, therefore, that once an agent has read and enjoyed the opening chapters within your initial submission, the next step for them is to call or email you and ask to read your full manuscript. And the best way to retain the momentum your opening chapters have just built for your manuscript is to be able to send it to them immediately. Essentially they want to see if your writing continues to hit the mark throughout the rest of the book. They'll also have read through the synopsis you provided, so with that outline of your plot in mind they'll consider the overarching shape of your narrative and whether it's as satisfying as it should be. In their opinion, scenes might need to move, a character culled, or lines of dialogue tweaked to help the words of your protagonist reverberate more throughout the core of the story. These are the sort of things they'll raise in a meeting or phone call with you if they remain interested in offering representation after reading the full manuscript.

If you don't have a complete manuscript ready to send to an agent upon request then, obviously, you're left with no other option than to make them wait. Which they probably will do (there's a reason they felt moved to ask if they could read more in the first place), but the passing of time may see their excitement wane as a result. (And in the meantime, could they have taken on another author writing in the same area as you?)

NON-FICTION

If you're writing memoir, then it's likely that you'll need to, yes. (Always take the time to check guidelines, however, because agencies can differ in what they ask for.) These books require a strong narrative structure and a distinctive tone of voice so, editorially, are treated more or less in the same way as fiction titles. However, the unique nature and authenticity of the author does become a factor in a publisher's decision to acquire a book of this type. This isn't about the author being 'well known', more about whether the book offers a wider audience something remarkable and/or relatable?

The balance definitely tips towards how recognisable an author's name is where autobiography is concerned, though, and it's therefore highly unlikely a manuscript needs to be finished at the point of submitting to agents. (In fact, it could be that an agent approaches the author if they're particularly well known.) Although celebrity autobiographies have recently taken a bit of a dive in popularity, the main reason publishers will always acquire them is because they can be fairly confident they'll get their money back (and more) on their investment. The right author brings with him/her a fan base ready to buy the book, while further marketing and publicity can raise awareness among general readers (with press attention from serialisation rights a possibility). It's fair to assume, for example, that an agent or publisher wouldn't turn away the opportunity to publish David Attenborough's autobiography just because he'd only written the first two chapters!

A non-fiction book may also have a dependency on research being carried out (interviews, photography, trips to key locations) or timed to coincide with an upcoming event. A sample of writing is still required, but the chapter breakdown of the book is the most important thing in grabbing an agent's attention, and it'll be this that they work on with an author when approaching a publisher with a proposal, not the manuscript itself.

For writers of biography and non-narrative non-fiction projects, however, it's not often that a manuscript is expected to be finished ahead of submitting either to a literary agent, or even before an agent tries to sell the book to a publisher. This is because the rights to a lot of books in this area are sold on the strength of a proposal (with the chapter breakdown and author credentials both focused on in particular), with the standard of writing not necessarily an immediate concern. This is because the publishers know they have the resources to improve a manuscript should they need to. The authenticity, expertise and subject-specific recognition that come along with the author's credentials, however, are the unique aspects of a book that only the writer can bring, and ones that are key to marketing and publicity campaigns.

## Does my book need a title before I submit it?

Good titles do help sell books, which is why there can be so much deliberation regarding this topic between author, agent and all those involved at a publisher ahead of a publication date being confirmed and the design, marketing and publicity teams going to work.

Publishers try to ensure that a title works in tandem with the cover design to help create interest and draw people to a book, with stylistic decisions also based upon what works within the context of your target market. The title alone, however, can very much work as an immediate pitch of your book, hooking a reader's interest amidst the dozens of others on the shelf vying for their attention. Being intrigued by a title means a reader may pick up a book and read the back cover blurb, then read some reviews, the first page, and then go on and buy the book. *The Girl on the Train* (written by Paula Hawkins), for example, more or less exactly encapsulates what the book is about, drawing the prospective reader in, making them think; *What about the girl on the train? I wonder what happens to her. What does she do? Where is she going? I take the train to work every day – is this going to be something I can relate to?*

If you can't settle on a title for your book ahead of submitting to an agent, then just go with a working one. They need a name to help to hang your manuscript on. And as inferred above, not being dead-set on the name of your book does probably make things that little less painful should suggested changes come your way from either your agent or publishing house editor (if not both). It's part of their job to suggest alternatives if they don't think your title is strong enough, especially so in the case of the publishing house editor, who is likely to have listened to the thoughts of their sales and marketing departments as well. Where non-fiction is concerned, for example, a subtitle might be considered as a necessary way to more clearly spell out the benefits of a book to a reader. Generally speaking, once a publisher has acquired rights to your book, while your voice will definitely still be heard, they'll change a title if they think it'll increase the market appeal of your book. This might be a personal wrench to the writer, but it's a clear example of a book no longer completely belonging to you; your publisher has paid for the right to publish it, and they employ professionals who specialise in producing and marketing books for your target readership. Their expertise is definitely something to carefully consider.

## When's the best time to send a submission?

It's a fair question to ask, especially given that serendipity sometimes has a say in the chances of a book going on to be published. This is because there are so many external variables that your manuscript has to contend with. Are you catching an agent at a time when they're feeling really positive and want to get their teeth into a project exactly like yours? Or do you have the most brilliant manuscript but it faces really stiff competition in a part of the market that's become saturated? Even some books that have gone on to become international bestsellers have struggled to find a home initially, so you have to be prepared to go through something similar. Is it a case of your manuscript not quite being ready? Or do you continue to plug away, convinced by the quality of your writing and it's simply a case of it not being picked up by an agent that sees its potential?

'*But is there an* optimum *time to send my submission?*' you cry. Maybe mid-afternoon, when admin tasks are in hand and an agent has just returned to their desk with a cup of tea? That definitely sounds better than sending it late at night and being caught up with all of the other post-5.30pm emails that an agent has to read when they arrive at their desk the following morning. But then what if you're submitting to an agent who always gets to the office by 7am because it gives them a couple of hours of uninterrupted reading time? Maybe that gives your late evening submission more of a chance? And what about over Christmas? Will the agent you're querying turn on their Out Of Office from 20th December onwards, or does their train home get delayed on Christmas Eve and they have nothing to do other than read through recent submissions? All of these scenarios are possible but so are their direct opposites, so it's more or less impossible to second-guess. All you can control is your professional approach to the process of submitting your work, and the quality of your writing.

Although that 'perfect time to submit' is always going to remain elusive, there's a bit more certainty in identifying particular times *not* to send agents your work. Submitting either in the fortnight leading up to one of the international book fairs or during the following 'recovery week' can decrease the likelihood of your work being read anytime soon. Why not keep an eye on the start- and end-dates of London, Bologna (if you're writing for children) and Frankfurt Book Fairs and check against them before preparing to submit? Not allowing your manuscript to get swept away in the stress, admin, contracts and general exhaustion of an agent before/after these events could mean they approach it in a more positive frame of mind in general.

SEE ALSO *Is attending book fairs a good way to get an agent?* page 43 and *What's the most efficient way of submitting my manuscript?* page 92.

# Should I submit to multiple agents at the same time?

It's absolutely fine to send your submission to more than one agent. They expect you to have approached one or more of their peers, and competition is considered healthy. If an agent shows an interest in your work and asks to read the full manuscript, some could ask for a short period of exclusivity but most simply ask that, out of courtesy, you make them aware of any interest shown by another agent.

Sending out your work to small batches of agents at the same time could be a smart approach, although make sure to keep everyone you've submitted to informed of any developments (such as full-read requests, meetings and/or offers of representation). This is a moment of leverage that's to your benefit, though, as it can be used to speed up the process of agents coming back to you. Let's say, for example, you've submitted your book to five agents and received a rejection letter from two but a full-read request from the third agent to respond. At this point, even if it's well within the expected response times outlined in each of the remaining agents' submission guidelines, it's perfectly reasonable for you to contact the remaining two agents to let them know; just take care to keep the tone of this email one of a polite chaser (*'Dear Agent X, Just a quick email to let you know an agent at Agency Name has asked to read the manuscript in full. Best, Name'*) rather than something that passive-aggressively suggests they need to hurry up.

A polite email update regarding a show of interest in your work indicates a writer who's courteous, professional and, crucially, someone who's written something of a high enough quality to warrant the time of a peer operating in their part of the market to request to read it in full. All of which may be enough to bump their submission up towards the top of an agent's To Read pile. One thing *not* to do, however, is to use this tactic as a means of speeding things up. Claiming interest from other agents might initially have the desired effect but it won't be that long before you're rumbled. The publishing industry is deceptively small when you begin to boil it down by the number of people working on your type of book, making the chances of everyone at least knowing of one another quite high. *'Did your colleague at Agency X really show an interest in Book Y? The author sent it to me as well, then followed up with an email to say they'd had a meeting request ... but when I read the opening chapters I really didn't like the writing. I'm a bit confused because it doesn't seem like the sort of thing that would be up Agent Z's street ...'* As soon as your name becomes linked with this sort of scenario it becomes a lot more difficult for any agent to imagine striking up a trusting relationship with you.

On the subject of agents talking to one another about the sort of manuscript submissions they've received of late, also avoid querying two agents at the same agency with the same book. If a book isn't for Agent A but they think it might be of interest to their colleagues, then chances are they'll pass it on.

One final thing to avoid: resist the temptation to use the same covering letter to submit to multiple agents. Impersonal covering letters are held in the same regard as one of those pieces of marketing that lands on your doormat from an estate agent or energy supplier: it's addressed to you, but then you quickly realise it's not *really* for you, and your eyes glaze over as a result. As a writer, are you really not bothered about who acts on the behalf of you and your writing? And then even worse than this is to copy all of the agents in on your email, brazenly setting each agent up in competition with one another and confirming a lack of regard for each of them in one fell swoop.

SEE ALSO *What's the most efficient way of submitting my manuscript?* page 92 and *Do I need to write bespoke covering letters to each agent?* page 98.

## Is it possible to have more than one literary agent?

If you are writing in two disciplines and those disciplines are distinct enough, then a second agent might be necessary. For example, if you've established a career as a literary novelist it could be that the agent representing you doesn't have any interest in being able to represent a book on gardening you'd like to publish. In this case, so long as you can assure both agents (and publishers if you secure deals for both books) that you're able to meet the demands of both projects, this shouldn't be much of an issue. Should you be a crime novelist wanting to find a publisher for a historical romance, however, your original agent could feel they are able to represent both books.

A note of caution to end on, though. It's far from uncommon for writers to have lots of book ideas tucked up their sleeve, and for these not all to be in the same genre. Once you secure an agent, they're very likely to advise you against making a jump into a different genre with your next book, particularly if you're writing fiction. This is not to be dismissive of a project, just that it's better to prioritise a follow-up more likely to help you establish a readership.

SEE ALSO *What are co-agents?* page 221.

## Can I send more than one book to an agent in the same submission?

If you're seeking representation for a full-length fiction or non-fiction project, then no. The primary focus of your submission should be on one book only, the opening chapters of which should be attached. Don't confuse things by attaching anything to do with another book, even if you have a series of books planned. It doesn't matter how much work you've put into mapping out – or even writing – a fantasy trilogy, all you can do is submit the first in the series and hope the agent in question expresses an interest. The same goes for a book in which you introduce a recurring protagonist along the lines of Jason Bourne.

It does make sense, however, to include a sentence in your covering letter that informs a prospective agent the next book you're working on is one that's going to appeal to the same type of audience as your first.

If you're writing picture books, then while making sure the focus of your submission is one story in particular, it could be that you're encouraged to send others too. This isn't just because they're easy to read through and assess quickly, but because there's an expectation that children's picture book authors are relatively prolific in their output (parents tend to want to buy more than one if the author is a hit at home). Publishers know this so are more inclined to take an author on if they know that the writer has more books lined up and ready to go.

## I've co-written a book with another writer. Does that change anything?

It shouldn't do, and if it does then you just haven't found the right agent to represent you.

There's some logic to agents and publishers perhaps being cautious about the potential for complications that could arise from dealing with two authors, but provided it's clear you're both contributing towards producing great manuscripts, that's all that matters.

Also, remember that the secondary purpose of a covering letter is to give an agent a sense of you as a writer. As such, and because co-authors aren't that common, you should make sure to be very clear about this creative arrangement from the outset.

## Should I submit my work under a pen name?

No, because it could get you off on the wrong foot with an agent. An agent will offer a representation agreement only after a meeting to discuss your book in greater depth (both the manuscript itself, and also where they see it fitting into the wider marketplace). This meeting also provides an opportunity to get a sense of what it's going to be like working with you, and it's unlikely to go down as a great start to your professional relationship if you're forced to admit that you answer to a different name. In short, is submitting under a pen name a decision that promotes a trust between you and a potential agent?

Instead, why not sidestep any awkwardness and just mention in your covering letter that you intend to write under a *nom de plume*? Discussing the possibility of doing so would definitely be something your prospective agent would be happy to talk about within a pre-representation agreement meeting. This seems to be a better solution than risking your potential working relationship beginning quite awkwardly.

## I'm a UK-based author. Can I submit to US agents?

By all means, but ask yourself the following before you do:

1.  is your target market in the US or UK?
2.  how often will you see your agent if they're based in the US?

Both questions are worth considering because the way they're answered relates to the effectiveness of the submissions you're sending out, and also your experience of the author-agent relationship if you do go on to become represented. Are you comfortable in mostly being in touch with your agent online? This might not be a problem for some, but for other people it could prove to be a drawback. Is there a greater demand within the US market for the book you've written? If so, it could well be the right decision as a US agent probably stands a much better chance of securing a good deal for your book with their publishing contacts. However, if a US publisher isn't totally sure about acquiring your book, could being based in the UK work against you? How available would you be for promotional opportunities, for example? And how expensive would it be to fly an unheralded author to and from the country? If budgets are tight (and they often are) then these factors will be considered.

## Can I submit my book to film/TV agents *and* a literary agent?

Technically yes, but it's likely you're trying to run before you can walk. Firstly, are you a screenwriter or an author? Next, do you have a submission you honestly believe is strong enough in both mediums (when both require such different approaches to storytelling)? And finally, if your book gets published, sells well and captures the eye of a film or TV producer, your literary agent is there to help you take advantage of the opportunity (although realistically, the number of books that actually get optioned and then go on to be adapted are probably not as high as you'd hope).

If dreams of your book being adapted for film or TV help get you through some of the tougher moments when writing early drafts then that's fine, but don't lose sight of the fact you're the writer of a *book*. Don't forget that literary agents first priority is prose, and therefore consider any film or TV adaptations a long way in the distance until your book is published and a hit with readers.

## Can I submit my book to an agent if I write poetry?

There are plenty of ways to get single poems published but, such is the relatively low demand for poetry anthologies within the current marketplace, poets don't tend to have agents. Or if they do, it's because they're working on a prose project (full-length fiction or non-fiction).

There are always exceptions to this, but in general poetry anthologies acquired by publishers are those from a recognised name in the field.

Poets can build their reputation on a poem-by-poem basis by having their work published in pamphlets, journals, magazines or websites respected in the poetry community: some offer payment for the poems they choose to publish, though this can lead to an entry fee being charged for competitions. The *Writers' & Artists' Yearbook* lists these, though also consult The Poetry Library and poetrymagazines.org. uk. Getting a handle on these different outlets and submitting work to them obviously provides good practice in adhering to submission guidelines (word count, writing to a certain style or theme, and working to a deadline). And if your work is regularly published, it's more likely that you'll be noticed by agents. Being placed in poetry competitions, gaining a scholarship or performing poetry are other ways to bring your work to people's attention, as well as impressive things to add to any covering letter. Realistically, though, that covering letter might pack more of a punch if it concerns prose you have written rather than poetry.

## Can I submit my book to an agent if I write short stories?

Even if an agent wanted to lead their approach of editors with one of unpublished clients' short story collections, the reality is (due to relatively limited market demand) they'd find it a difficult sell. A few success stories are all that's needed to change momentum, though, and who's to say the winds of change are not blowing right now? George Saunders built a career from writing short stories long before his first novel won the Booker Prize in 2017; while Kristen Roupenian's *Cat Person*, a short story published in the New Yorker that proceeded to go viral, saw her receive a seven-figure advance for her debut novel that published in 2018. Yet the more general state of play is that, even though they may be drawn to a writer after enjoying a short story published in a magazine or one that's been ranked highly in a competition they've been on the judging panel for, most agents are unlikely to offer a short-story writer representation on the promise of short stories alone. A long-form fiction or non-fiction project is going to be of greater immediate interest, though striving to get short stories published in recognised magazines or as prize-winning competition entries can only help you build a reputation as a talent agents will be interested to work with.

## How do I know if I'm writing 'literary', 'commercial' or 'genre' fiction?

This can be a bit of a grey area as it comes down to interpretation, while the term 'literary–commercial crossover' further blurs the lines. Is it about the prose, the content, or just down to the marketing departments? And aren't all novels commercial?

As noted earlier, a 'literary' novel tends to be considered as such because it explores a protagonist's emotional journey and there's a more abstract approach to the themes central to the narrative. A novel classed as 'commercial', however, is considered to be plot driven, while 'genre fiction' often takes this same approach (with leading characters driving the book forward) but also conforms to particular traits readers of a particular genre are familiar with (romance and crime novels are good examples).

But don't all works of fiction contain a bit of both? Genre fiction is more than likely to have wider themes at play (love, tragedy, religion, morality) while most literary novels do need to hinge on a plot moving the story forward. Perhaps the emphasis placed upon these particular narrative devices is what leads to a book being classified in one camp rather than the other.

Some books, however, give enough weight to aspects from both the literary and commercial toolbox: a difficult balance to strike, but ultimately has a chance of appealing to a much wider reading audience.

Examples of authors who have had success with 'literary–commercial crossover' fiction ('Upmarket fiction' is a term that's been used in the US), are Ali Smith, Donna Tartt, Ian McEwan, Cormac McCarthy and Audrey Niffenegger. Each has produced books that appeal to the general book-buying public looking for a story to discuss at work or with their friends, and also receive the acclaim of being nominated for literary prizes.

## Is it more difficult to get an agent with a cross-genre novel?

Are you an optimist or a pessimist? If you're an optimist, then you might consider your cross-genre novel to be one that has the potential to combine two audiences, and opens up double the number of prospective agents to seek representation with.

A pessimist, though, can spot potential flaws in this way of thinking. Does your book really do enough to appeal to readers of both genres? Or will an agent see you as someone trying to be a jack of all trades when they'd much prefer a master of one?

Getting beta readers to interrogate whether your claims of having written a cross-genre novel carry weight could be invaluable as you begin to prepare your submission documents to send off to agents. In which part of a bookstore would they place your book if it was published? If there's a murder in your book, is that enough to go on and state 'it contains elements that would appeal to fans of crime/thriller'? Or is it just a plot point within a work of historical fiction? Honest answers to these sorts of questions should go a long way to helping you decide whether referring to the book as appealing to readers of a single genre might make for a stronger pitch.

Perhaps a wider question to ask if you're starting to worry about any of this, though, is whether it's worth getting bogged down in bookseller jargon? This is essentially what terms like 'cross-genre' or 'commercial-literary crossover' are, and incidental to the primary focus of an agent, whose major concern is: Is the writing any good? You do need to have an idea of who your book appeals to, but it's of much greater importance to ensure your concept is an intriguing one, your reader feels compelled to turn the page, and your narrative voice is one that engages.

## Why do some agents stop accepting submissions?

This could be for any number of reasons, and an example of why it's essential to keep an eye on an agent's social media profile and/or their page on their agency website ahead of sending your book out to them. Checking these sources for information might give you a better idea of how long they won't be accepting submissions. Is it a temporary measure because they're away? Are they moving agencies? Or are they retiring or changing careers entirely? Perhaps they're going on maternity leave? Maybe they have so much work on with their existing list of clients that they just don't have space to add another writer to their list at this point. All of which you need to take on board and shift your focus to another agent on your 'target list' accordingly.

SEE ALSO *Why do authors and agents part company?* page 212.

## What does accepting 'on referral only' mean?

This is basically the opposite of an unsolicited manuscript, and a stipulation usually put in place by agents who have reached capacity in terms of the number of authors they're able to represent. Another reason an agent might do this is to reduce the number of submissions they're dealing with in order to refocus their list; maybe moving away from a genre because they're overstocked or market demand has fallen.

Manuscript submissions only being considered 'on referral only' means an agent is only willing to look at manuscripts recommended to them by someone they know. This could be an agency reader, one of their authors, an editor or another industry contact – all people likely to be aware of their writing tastes, and whose opinion they trust.

## Should I submit to a new or more established agent?

As we've touched on already, there are pros and cons in both instances to bear in mind, though in either case they should remain incidental to what really matters: have you found the right agent to champion your book? Writing a book and finding an agent to represent it is hard, so if an agent's literary tastes line up to the manuscript you've written then why discriminate?

In doing your research use the *Writers' & Artists' Yearbook*, use Twitter, use Google and YouTube to read and watch agent interviews, as well as paying attention to recently published books that have done well in your corner of the market. Working in this way means it shouldn't be too long before you're left with a list of agents to approach: some relatively new to the role (albeit with an industry background, such as in the rights or editorial departments of a publisher, or having been at an agency to gain experience) and with only a few clients to their name; and some who have been in the business for ten years and up.

It's only natural to start taking the extent of someone's know-how into consideration at this stage, but it shouldn't cloud your judgement too much: young or old, masses of expertise or just a handful of clients, if there's something about an agent that gives you the sense that they'll love your writing then you're doing yourself a disservice if you don't send it their way.

The team of editors responsible for compiling the Listings sections of the *Writers' & Artists' Yearbook* have taken the decision to back up this stance. All contact information for literary agencies is presented as objectively as possible: there's a word limit, large agencies appear in the same format as those that are more boutique, and newly formed agencies sit alongside companies founded decades ago. Agencies based in London are also not listed any differently to those elsewhere in the UK.

## WORKING WITH AN 'ESTABLISHED' LITERARY AGENT

Being represented by someone with a strong list of authors means you benefit from that agent's obvious experience. Great confidence should be taken in their desire to represent your writing; their existing responsibilities would no doubt have made it much easier to turn your book away, so your work must have real appeal. But while it's a huge compliment for an agent with a healthy list of authors to have made time for you and your book, inextricably linked to this comes a potential fly in the ointment: how much of their time will they be able to devote to you? Pay close attention to agent's lists, as they could be misleading. How often are their authors having work published (i.e., does their list contain research-intensive nonfiction authors or enigmatic literary fiction novelists)? Does that list include author estates? Does it include debut authors whose books are yet to publish? As an inexperienced author, there's little doubt you're going to benefit from your agent's writing guidance, industry knowhow, and proven ability to broker deals with publishers, but it's important to recognise that every author they represent generates work: new drafts submitted, publicity schedule queries, rights to sell, editorial concerns, royalty statements to chase and more. Among all of this, what about the development of *your* manuscript? In discussing how you might work with one another during a pre-representation meeting, why not take the opportunity to find out more about how often you might meet your agent ahead of Book One being published? Would you be more than happy to work on the basis of only being available to meet with your agent every few months? This might suit some writers more than others, and is worth bearing in mind ahead of sending off your submission.

WORKING WITH A 'NEW' LITERARY AGENT

Just because an agent is developing a client list, it doesn't mean they are inexperienced. They are highly likely to have been around the publishing industry for a significant period of time, just not as a literary agent outright. Their previous role, for example, could have been as a reader within an agency before working their way up, or in the rights or editorial team at a publishing house. Could their knowledge of working on the other side of the industry offer you access to great contacts, and therefore make the difference in getting the best deal for your book?

One other reason not to discriminate against getting in touch with agents who appear relatively inexperienced is the excellent advantage of linking up your writing and beginnings of your career with the time they'll have for you and their hunger to succeed. With fewer authors to occupy them, the chances are greater of one-to-one editorial advice as well as general availability throughout when it comes to dealing with publishers or attending writing or industry-centric events for the first time. This might be the sort of reassurance and guidance that's crucial to building your confidence as you make the transformation from aspiring writer to published author.

SEE ALSO *What sort of things should I ask if I meet a literary agent?* page 184.

# What's the most efficient way of submitting my manuscript?

Be organised, send out small waves of submissions (say to a group of five agents, then wait for their responses), and keep your ear to the ground. Obviously this doesn't mean sending *exactly* the same submission to each agent in the group. You should still tailor your covering letters accordingly, as outlined above.

A spreadsheet can be a useful and relatively simple way to keep track of the agents you've approached. It can also help you manage your own expectations, and that's vital if you are to stave off frustration and be realistic about wait-times for agent responses. Use it to note down the date you send your work to each agent. Then create another column next to this that contains the date by which you should expect to hear from each agent. This should be easy to find, given most agency guideline pages state an approximate turnaround time for unsolicited submissions. Seeing these dates in black and white should hopefully be enough to prevent you from following up your submission email with another along the lines of 'Just checking if you've received this', or making a phone call to the office. You're perfectly entitled to send a polite chaser email, though, if you haven't received a reply from an agent within their suggested response time (which tends to be between six to eight weeks, as noted, but always check individual agency guidelines as they do vary).

Sending out submissions in small batches is certainly worth considering, as it gives you the chance to reflect on and actually apply any feedback you might get. If you've made a glaring mistake, for example, or a couple of agents have come back to you to say the writing is great in sections but they didn't find the opening quite engaging enough, then you've provided yourself with a chance to make any changes you feel are necessary before sending out to another small group of agents. You could begin by, for example, organising potential agents by order of preference based on the research you've done.

SEE ALSO *Should I submit to multiple agents at the same time?* page 80.

## A FINAL NOTE ON RESEARCH ...

Before we move onto the practicalities of putting together a submission package, one final note on research. While the writing and concept of your book should remain your absolute priority, researching the current marketplace and the agents who might show an interest in representing your work should be second on your To Do list. For your book to have a chance of reaching its potential (and beyond!), you need to know a bit about the other titles it's competing against. What does your book do differently and why should readers buy it? Next, who seem to be the best agents to represent it? Search in the latest edition of the *Writers' & Artists' Yearbook*, on agency websites, in the Acknowledgements pages of contemporary titles, on Twitter, and so on; in truth, finding out a bit more about literary agent tastes has never been easier for writers, so try to take advantage.

And this sort of research may have the added bonus of you being able to more easily compose a bespoke, professional covering letter, a document that's a fork in the road between 'just' writing and entering the business of being a writer. To write a covering letter is to say:

'I've written something I think is good enough for a publisher to invest in.'

And to the recipient it should say:

'I've looked into the writers you represent and the books you're looking for and believe you to be the best person to act on my behalf in approaching publishers with my work.'

Only by setting some time aside to research agents can you be sure you're meeting these expectations (and therefore showing your writing the respect it deserves).

# The covering letter: dos and don'ts

A very high percentage of fiction writers – even the most revered – will have had to write a letter to an agent that introduces their book. A lot of authors writing popular non-fiction will have had to do the same, too. Writing a covering letter has long been established as part of the process of asking a literary agent to consider your work, and while some might find it an onerous task, whichever way you look at it, it's a necessary one. In fact, it's as necessary as working on a CV in the hope of being invited for a job interview.

The aim of this section is to provide the Dos and Don'ts of writing a covering letter; flagging mistakes to avoid and highlighting what could improve your chances of making a positive first impression with the agent you're querying. First, though, it's important to put the task of writing the letter into perspective. Assuming you produce something that's coherent, a covering letter will never be the key deciding factor in an agent expressing interest in your book or not. For authors of fiction, getting across the concept of your book and displaying the quality of your writing within your opening chapters is the most important thing. Next, the full manuscript needs to be complete. Then you need to put time into researching the agent(s) you're querying and having a grasp of your part of the marketplace. *Only then* does the covering letter come into the reckoning because without any of the aforementioned, your covering letter won't have the impact you were hoping for. (As mentioned previously, non-fiction authors will need to provide a writing sample and either a synopsis or more extensive chapter outline.)

In terms of the letter itself, you're looking to provide a window through which an agent can get a glimpse of your book, and also a sense of what it might be like to work with you; a one-page document that contains the following headline information:

- what you're submitting;
- why you're submitting it to that agent in particular;
- and a bit of relevant background about you.

It should be polite and professional in tone. It shouldn't be over-complicated; keep it as succinct as possible in order to let the writing within those opening pages do all the talking on your behalf.

That's easier said than done, perhaps, but if you know your book and can articulate concisely and invitingly what it is, who it's for and why it will appeal to a particular reading audience, then your letter has served its purpose, namely to make the agent you're querying want to set everything else aside and turn to your opening pages.

## Why is a covering letter necessary?

Because it gives an agent the information they need about your book before reading the sample chapters. What does the book hold? Who is it for? Why might it be of interest to them? Who are you?

It's easy for writers to forget two things: first, agents can receive dozens of submissions each week; and second, by and large, they approach each of these with genuine optimism. They *want* to find an exciting new talent who produces writing they enjoy.

The reason the covering letter is part of the protocol in putting together a submission (or non-fiction proposal) is that it helps an agent get into the mindset of what they're about to begin reading. Where your book is concerned, an agent doesn't get a recommendation from a mate, a cover design to spike their imagination or to read a review in a newspaper. All they have to go on before turning to your first page is the covering letter, which is why they expect it to give them an idea of what the writing is about and the style the author is trying to achieve. All of which constitutes the first piece of your prose an agent will read. Why not, then, view this as an opportunity rather than a challenge or a chore? Use the covering letter to frame your book in a way that does it justice, and introduce yourself in a professional manner.

## Is the covering letter *that* important?

It's not as important as your book or the market awareness that should've informed your decision to query the agent in the first place. As it's a requirement of a submission package, though, why not get it right? What's your book about? Why have you written it? Who's going to read it? Who are you?

If for whatever reason you're finding your letter difficult to write, don't spend hours and hours obsessing over getting it right. It's not *the thing*. Your book is *the thing*. Spend your hours getting that right instead. All that's expected of a covering letter is for you to present your book in an intriguing way, that you're courteous to the agent you're querying, and that you present yourself as an author committed to writing professionally.

## Why is a covering letter hard to write?

It shouldn't be if you know what makes your book tick and you stick to what the agent wants to know. It doesn't need to be a work of art. Accuracy and brevity are good tactics to employ, helping your writing and book idea remain the sole focus. Put forward what's at the core of your book and give it a chance to breathe. Leave it to the agent to get in touch if they have any further questions.

Also, some reassuring context. Agents often completely empathise with writers who get stuck in a rut with the covering letter because they're expected to produce them as part of pitching their clients' work to commissioning editors. Sometimes it flows better than others, but you always need to get the core information on the page.

## Do I need to write bespoke covering letters to each agent?

Yes. But there's no need to view this as an onerous task when there are so many positive reasons to put some time into tailoring a covering letter to each agent you approach for representation.

Just think about how you react to receiving marketing materials or updates from your bank or insurance provider. Even though the letter you open has been sent to your home address and the salutation uses your name, you *know* the personal nature of the content stops there. Your eyes glaze over and you have to force yourself to take the information in. Why, after all the time you've spent finessing your manuscript, do yourself this sort of injustice?

We've already covered this above, but it's worth repeating here: in terms of professional etiquette, one of the worst things you could do is to copy in all of the agents you're querying into the same email, (thus presenting them all with a generic covering letter and your synopsis and opening chapters attached). This is not OK. Every agent copied in will immediately see you as lazy, quite rude, and basically someone not particularly bothered about finding the right home for their manuscript. Is this the sort of person they're going to want to work with on a professional basis? No.

A bespoke covering letter is much more indicative of a writer who cares about their work. It shows you've actually thought about who might be the best person to represent what you've written, and it puts you in good stead with the agent you're querying because they'll be able to tell you've researched them and their list. And the very fact you've done this gives the impression you value your writing. You don't want it to be represented by just anyone, you want to work with someone you're likely to gel with creatively, and this is important when it comes to rounds of editorial work and, further down the line, when the agent begins championing your book to editors at potential publishers.

## What should a covering letter include?

It should be clear now that the job of your covering letter is to help the agent to whom you're submitting form a clear picture of the book you've written, and also gain a positive impression of what it might be like to work with you. Here are some things a good covering letter should include:

- salutation, including the agent's name, correctly spelled;
- framing devices – book title, word count, genre and/or intended reading audience, suitable comparisons if relevant (literary or otherwise);
- your pitch. What's at the heart of your book? What is its USP? Why would someone want to read it?
- Information about you – name, contact details, any relevant writing experience, anything else of interest that's relevant to your book. Mention formal writing qualifications (a recognised course, something previously published or shortlisted) if you have them, but there's no need to say you *don't* have any experience;
- agent-specific reasoning. Why have you sent your work to them? Are you aware of (and admire) some of the authors they represent? Have you met them at an event or follow them on Twitter and felt encouraged to send your work to them?
- politeness. This is a minimum expectation in forming a good working relationship;
- confidence. Believe in your book! If you don't, why should anyone else?

- professionalism. Adhere to submission guidelines, use a spellchecker, etc.

- brevity. Less is more. The covering letter is a *preamble* to the beginning of your manuscript. Let the manuscript do all the talking on your behalf.

### THINGS *NOT* TO INCLUDE IN A COVERING LETTER

What follows is a quick-fire list of common mistakes writers make within their covering letter to literary agents.

- 'Dear Sirs'. Tailor your covering letter to individual agents; don't 'Send To All'; and definitely do not assume every agent you submit to is a man because most are not.

- Referring to one's self. Don't leave out your contact details (email and phone number); it's a risk to sign your letter off using a *nom de plume*; and would you write any other application in the third person?

- Mistakes. If you're sloppy in your covering letter, then even before they've started reading your opening chapters an agent will have begun to wonder about the amount of editorial time they'll need to spend on your manuscript.

- Arrogance/unrealistic expectations. Is your book really going to be the next multi-million-selling phenomenon? Is it really your place to say it's better than the work of an acclaimed author? And don't mistake having an appreciation of the marketplace as an excuse to do someone else's job for them. There's no need for statistics, graphs or tables around the potential marketability of your book.

- Apologies. Don't be self-deprecating or dismissive of your work before an agent has even read the first page.

- Waffle. Don't overload an agent with lots of details about the book; don't include superfluous information about yourself ('I have two children and three dogs, Their names are …'); and don't waste words with statements like 'I've always written since I was a child'. Anyone could say that; what can you say that's remarkable?

- Gimmicks. Your manuscript submission should stand out for your writing only (although a solid proposal could be enough for non-narrative non-fiction writers). Don't undermine it with other 'features', such as wacky fonts, bullet-pointed lists, accompanying gifts, photos of yourself, illustrations, and similar.

- Lies. You'll get found out if you make a claim about your book that's untrue, and ruin any chance of trust with a prospective agent.

In isolation, one of the above errors is probably not going to mean an agent doesn't look at your sample section of writing. A clutch of these sorts of mistakes, however, is likely to make the agent wonder about whether they could work with you.

## How long should a covering letter be?

Guidelines usually state no more than a page, so around 400 words. Do your absolute best to stick to this but ... if you find that your letter is going to creep over by a couple of sentences, provided you're convinced you've been as succinct as possible, just click 'Send'. Most agents would rather read an extra twenty words than for a writer to start narrowing margins or reducing line-spacing and type size to keep everything on a single side.

## How should I format my covering letter?

As the guidelines on the submissions page of the agency website states. A standard request would be for it to be either an attachment or appear in the body of your email, and written in an easy-to-read 12-point font. Each agency could have slightly different requirements though, so check before sending to avoid making silly mistakes.

Also note that – particularly if asked to submit an introduction in the body of an email or via a form built into an agency website – the phrase 'covering letter' has been carried over from when submissions were all sent by post. The standard letter format (sender's address to the right margin, the recipients to the left) is therefore unnecessary; just think of the covering letter as a short email introducing your book.

Finally, while an agent can obviously hit 'Reply' to your query email, it's not uncommon for some to want to call and discuss things if they're interested in working with you. It's therefore worth including your contact telephone number beneath your name when you sign off.

## Is there a general structure to a covering letter?

There's not really an entirely 'set' template for writing a covering letter because it needs to take the mould of whatever you believe to be the best way to present you and your book, and any specific agency requests. Once you break down the key pieces of information an agent needs, though, then a useful quick-view structure does appear:

Dear Agent Name

Paragraph one: What it's called, Who it's for, Why it's for them

Paragraph two: About the book

Paragraph three: About you

Writer Name

SEE ALSO *The covering letter: examples and exercises* page 125.

## Should I write my letter in the voice of my protagonist?

It's a risk, especially when there is no expectation for the covering letter to be anything other than an introduction to you and your manuscript. You absolutely *do not* want an agent to have to work hard at understanding what they're about to begin reading. Do you think you're honestly going to be able to provide information about yourself, mention reasons why you're submitting to the agent, and also relay your book's intended audience all in the voice of your protagonist? It seems an unnecessarily high-wire act.

If you think your narrative style or voice of your protagonist is particularly distinctive (and therefore essential to hooking an agent's attention), go with your gut instinct and find a way to include it. But rather than committing to writing the entire letter in this way, why not just use a short sentence or two from your manuscript and include it at the beginning of the letter? If this is impactful and serves to take an agent straight to the heart of your book, it could be a good technique to employ.

## Should I sign off my letter from my author alias?

Unless there's an obviously understandable reason to want to conceal your identity (you're a published author looking to write in a completely different genre, or you're a 'celebrity' and want objective feedback on your work), don't do this. It's much better to show total trust in the working relationship you're hoping to have with the agent you're approaching for representation, rather than setting yourself up for a potentially awkward explanation when meeting them for the first time ('Actually, my name's not Keith, it's John.'). Writing under a *nom de plume* is definitely something an agent (and hopefully a publisher) will be open to discussing but, until then, just concentrate on being transparent and building a professional relationship with the person you're hoping will act on your behalf.

## Do I tell an agent I've paid an editor to look at my manuscript?

There is no expectation from an agent that a writer should pay for an editing service. If you have done, though, it is useful background information to include towards the end of your covering letter.

Someone working to industry standards has assessed (and may even have endorsed) your writing and, assuming you've re-worked your manuscript based on their suggestions, an agent will turn to your opening chapters hopeful of the writing being of a particularly high standard.

Yet while paying for an editor to look at your work shows commitment to improving your manuscript, some agents could wonder about the level of the writing before that intervention and the amount of editorial support they might have to invest in the future.

## How much biographical information should I include?

Other than your name, where you live and what you do, stick to information that's relevant to your writing. Don't make the mistake of talking more about yourself than your book.

It's difficult to be too prescriptive about the information you decide to include in your covering letter, though, as what's 'relevant' for you depends very much on what your book's about and what makes you tick as an author. For example, it would normally be considered over the top to list the name of your three cats in your covering letter … but if you've written a book *about* cats it might make a lot more sense for this detail to be included.

The only other biographical information to consider including would be about an experience linked to your manuscript (thus giving your work greater authenticity), or any writing credentials you might have to speak of (previous publications, prizes, courses, etc.). However, and as noted above, writing qualifications aren't in any way expected. If you have them, great, but it's not the end of the world if you don't.

# Do I need to have any 'writing qualifications' to be considered by an agent?

The emphasis placed on your writing credentials differs slightly between writers of fiction and non-fiction.

### FICTION

Your background as a writer doesn't count for a great deal if you're writing fiction. All agents care about is the book. If that's engaging enough, whether you have a first-class degree from Oxford or no GCSEs at all, is all secondary. And the same goes for any writing courses, qualifications or editing services you've paid for. If you have them then they're probably relevant so mention them, but in the end this is no more or less impressive than getting up to write before a double shift. Being placed on a competition shortlist (or winning one!), as well as a testimonial from a recognised writer or industry professional could all serve to put your submission to the top of an agent's 'To read' pile, but that's as far as their influence goes. It all comes down to your opening three chapters in the end.

Finally, life experiences of particular relevance to your book carry just as much weight as a writing qualification. They add personality to your covering letter, and an authenticity to your book which could end up being discussed as a good marketing angle. Do you have primary experience of the situation or themes you're writing about? Did a quirk of your personal or professional life inspire the book you've written?

### NON-FICTION

While the quality of the writing obviously does matter, it's not the be all and end all for writers submitting non-fiction. In this case, the authenticity of an author is a selling point that carries greater weight with agents and publishers, particularly where non-narrative non-fiction books are concerned. If you're a recognised name in your field and have a good concept, then – with a small writing sample and a detailed chapter outline – this could be enough to convince a publisher to bid for the rights to your book because authenticity sells.

If you're writing *narrative* non-fiction, such as memoir, then the state of the manuscript will be judged a lot more carefully (the narrative arc and voice are just as intrinsic to this sort of book as they are for a piece of fiction), yet it will also be scrutinised alongside the following question: is your account both unique and relatable enough to be the one everyone wants to read?

To finish, a quick note on the importance that timing plays in non-fiction proposals. You have to be patient, organised and proactive as books can take up to two years to be published, so if you know a significant anniversary is coming up it's crucial to have your manuscript or proposal ready a long way in advance.

## Should I mention having tried and failed to seek representation before?

Opinion may differ on this, but it's probably best to leave this out of a covering letter. Yes, you might've previously received full manuscript requests and bespoke feedback from a number of agents (or you may even have been represented by an agent before), but why not hold any details like this back until you get to the stage of a pre-representation meeting with an agent?

## How much does my social media following matter?

Unless you have hundreds of thousands of followers, special dispensations are unlikely to be made for writers just because they have an active social media profile. It always comes down to the book. Reading within your genre, researching the agents you're going to approach and building a good knowledge of the industry and marketplace are on the next tier down, followed by your covering letter, then synopsis. Arguably social media comes after all of this (if at all, because not everyone uses it).

Obviously an active social media profile and an engaged audience is a good thing to have, and prospective publishers will see it as 'another way in' for readers, who tend to think along the lines of 'That book sounds quite interesting. I wonder what the author's like? Do they have a social media account? Do they have a website?'

This is actually the same sort of thought process some agents will follow, too. If they're interested in reading more than the opening you've submitted to them, before contacting you to read the full manuscript they might well type your name into Google and try to see if they can find a bit more out about you. Maybe you have a website or blog where you post about your writing process? Social media pages will appear in these results, too.

If having a social media profile isn't something you feel comfortable with, it's unlikely to affect things too much in terms of gaining representation. It shouldn't have a bearing on whether a publisher acquires your manuscript either, but it may be a conversation they're keen to have with you. It can be a way to have a voice beyond your books, and/or reaffirm your credentials as an expert in a particular field if you're writing non-fiction. And it's also important not to lose sight of how positive social media can be for writers. It's a tool you can use to network, find out more about agents, get book recommendations, pick up writing tips and maybe even find beta readers. Dipping your toe in the water to explore this could end up proving to be of great assistance.

# The covering letter: writing a pitch

Pitching is a part of life. Approaching your boss with a request or an idea is pitching. Trying to convince your friends which film to watch is pitching. Why should approaching an agent, who has dozens of other writers vying for their attention, to represent you be any different?

What's more, your pitch – a snappy sentence or two that encapsulates your book, and similar to the sort of thing you'd find on the back cover of a book – isn't just some sort of test to pass as part of the submission process. If your book is to go on and get published, it's something that's going to be used throughout that entire journey: from hooking an agent through to piquing the interest of a new reader. In short, a memorable pitch can help a book go a long way in a crowded marketplace. Go back to the last time you were browsing in a bookshop, for example, and the things that might have led you to picking up a book. Maybe an author's name in a window display took you back to a conversation with friends about what they've enjoyed reading of late. Maybe you were drawn in by a book's cover. Maybe it was down to store placement and a book being surrounded by other titles you recognise. Maybe there was a short review of the book written by one of the bookshop staff. Or were you simply intrigued by the title (arguably the very first pitch of your book)?

The title aside, none of the above is available to you when sending off your work to an agent. The pitch *is*, though. It's the one thing you can draw on in these early stages of trying to get published that can have a huge influence. Can you succinctly tell people what's at the heart of your book, hint at who it's for, and make them want to dive in? When someone asks 'What's your book about?', does your reply make them say 'Interesting! When can I read it?'?

# What is a pitch?

It's a concise, memorable sentence or two used to sell your book. It very succinctly conveys what the book is trying to be, giving a potential reader a flavour of what they're about to invest their time and (hopefully) money in. In fiction and memoir, the pitch needs to introduce the world of the book, the lead protagonist(s), and the conflict that drives the narrative forward. In non-narrative non-fiction, the pitch should give an idea of the concept of the book, the key information it contains and from what source. Remember to spell out the benefits of the book, too.

If your pitch does its job, then it will tell people what the book is about in a memorable but matter-of-fact way. Imagine someone you don't know asking you about what you do for a living at a party. For fear of boring them, you find the words to summarise what you do in the most relatable way. Can you apply the same skills to describing your book?

# Why is a pitch important?

First, it's not as important as the book. It might do a good job in bringing attention to a book that's not yet at a publishable standard, but if your aim is to secure the representation of an agent and then to be published, a pitch will only help you so far.

Assuming you've written a book that's a real contender, though, a good pitch can actually end up having a significant impact. It can make your book memorable, understandable and intriguing in one fell swoop. Its effectiveness doesn't just stop at grabbing the attention of an agent, either; books have to be 'sold' an awful lot of times before they end up in the hands of a reader.

- Your book pitch appears in your covering letter to a potential agent, who might have another 100 submissions to consider.

- Once you have an agent and your manuscript is 'submission ready', your agent will use your pitch (or a revised version of it) in their approach to editors. This could be in conversation and/or formally in a covering letter with your manuscript attached.

- If an editor loves your book, it becomes their job to 'sell' it to their colleagues. This means gaining the support of not just others in editorial, but also getting past an acquisitions committee that contains representatives from rights, sales and marketing departments. A version of your pitch is the most succinct way for them to do this.

- When a publisher acquires the book, they then have to convince booksellers and librarians to stock it. Again, the pitch is likely to be what they lead with.

- In advance of the book being available to general readers, the manuscript (and sometimes advance reader copies) goes out to reviewers. The pitch is likely to make an appearance here, and could form the basis of the blurb on the back of the book.

- Once the book is available to the book-buying public, any marketing and publicity campaigns arranged by the publisher are obviously designed to 'sell' your book to potential readers. There's a good chance a one-line version of your pitch will appear.

- Finally, booksellers need to find ways to sell books to customers, either through window, wall or aisle displays, special offers, or Staff Recommendation cards on shelves. Again, a one-line pitch could well play a part.

## Blurb, pitch, elevator pitch, synopsis ... what's the difference?

Writers can get confused by some of the jargon used within the submission process. And that's all too understandable, given that some of these words can be used interchangeably, while agents and editors can also be guilty of forgetting how industry-specific they are.

Basically, each of the below refers to different pieces of writing that relate to the manuscript or rather how it's sold or promoted to a variety of audiences. Each varies in length but there are two common denominators to bear in mind: first, they require the writer to pare their book back. It doesn't matter that a synopsis is one page long and a pitch is a couple of sentences, the expectation is that a book's driving force needs to be front and centre.

And second, being specific is crucial. If you're writing fiction, your synopsis is only ever going to fit on a single side of A4 if you concentrate solely on the actions of your protagonist and the central tension of your story. As soon as you start giving time to your secondary characters, you move away from what your reader (agent) wants. This same logic applies to writing a shorter pitch, too. To have any hope of boiling your book down to a couple of sentences, you need to focus on your leading character, the problem they face and/or the journey they go on.

**One-line pitch/logline:** Both terms are exactly as they sound, with the term 'logline' something that's borrowed from the film industry. And to continue in this vein, let's look at a fabled example of the one-line pitch said to have been used to sell the script for the 1979 film *Alien*: 'Jaws in space.' Just three words encapsulate exactly what the viewer is going to get. Can you do the same for your book?

Back to fiction writing, though. How about taking a look at your bookshelves for inspiration? A popular trend in fiction titles is to have a one-line pitch somewhere on the cover. *The Life Of Pi* is a good example: 'One boy, one boat, one tiger.' This offers intrigue, nods to there being fantastical elements to the novel, and basically gives the reader a flavour of the main ingredients they can expect from the spine of the book (including the dramatic tension of how a tiger becomes involved). As an exercise in exploring how to explain what's at the crux of your story, are you able to do something similar?

**Elevator pitch:** this is another term taken from the film industry that you might hear mentioned for illustrative purposes, largely because of the useful anecdote associated with it. You – the writer – are playing the part of a fledgling screenwriter waiting for a lift. By pure chance, just as the doors are closing, a famous producer gets in the lift with you. As you watch them select which floor they need to get off at, it dawns on you that this is your one chance to tell them about your screenplay.

It's easy to see, then, why agents can use this term to describe the pitch in the covering letter. In written form, can you put together something that's short, impactful, memorable and gets across the essence of your book as well as hinting at the sort of style it's been written in?

**The pitch:** this should appear in your covering letter, be no more than two to three sentences in length and set your book up for an agent. It's fine for you to use comparisons to other cultural touchstones within this section of writing. (Note that 'the pitch', like 'the proposal', can be used as a collective noun to refer to the entire set of documents that make up a submission.)

When writing a pitch, you should mention your book's title, its genre, the setting/time, introduce the central character and hint at the journey they're going to go on and/or the problem they're facing. Basically, you're trying to mention the who, what, where, when and why of your book (with the emphasis on this information perhaps shifting based on the type of book you're writing), and all as succinctly as possible. This should lead you towards a punchy, memorable summary that encapsulates what's at the nub of your book. After reading your pitch, without having read the manuscript, an agent should be able to 'place' what you've written and be captivated enough to want to open your first chapter to see how it unfolds.

**Blurb:** this is the piece of writing you find on the back of a book. It can be slightly longer than the pitch featured in a covering letter, and offer more information specific to the narrative. As such, it's less likely to include comparisons to other cultural touchstones as a means of describing the book.

**Synopsis:** this is a simple single-page document for everyone working on your book to use as a point of reference. If the job of your pitch is to sell your story, the job of a synopsis is to show how your story hangs together. You will only be asked formally to provide a synopsis as part of the submission process, but it can be an extremely useful document to produce during the writing process of planning, writing and re-drafting your book.

## What does 'USP' mean?

It's an abbreviation borrowed from the business world that's short for 'unique selling point'. Can you identify the one thing that makes your book stand apart from the competition? This is a really useful exercise to work through, particularly if you're writing a pitch for a piece of non-fiction. Is there an angle that only you can offer on a given subject? Do you have access to information (photographs, data, interviewees) that make your book of particular interest? If so, these are useful details to insert into your book proposal.

## How do I write a pitch?

As noted above, the best way to write a impactful pitch is to keep it exclusively about your main character, the situation they find themselves in and dilemma they face. A pitch is arguably not even a place for an explanation of the time and setting of a book, though these do tend to come through by association. Here are two examples of pitches to consider.

1. Set in mid-1950s, TITLE X is about a family struggling to heal the wounds inflicted upon them by the Second World War and deals with identity and loss.

2. Set in the mid-2000s, TITLE Y is a work of historical fiction that tells the story of CHARACTER 1 and her son, CHARACTER 2, who must flee the war-torn country of Iraq to search for the husband and father they have lost. But does he want to be found?

The difference between the two is specificity. TITLE X does tell us that it's about a family and gives us a sense of time and place, but nothing more than that. It's unremarkable (identity and loss are themes in countless novels) and won't elicit much more than a lukewarm response from a reader at the key moment of deciding whether or not to invest their time and money in the book. In terms of placing the book, TITLE X could be a piece of historical fiction, but it could also be a memoir, family saga, or maybe something for YA readers. As a result, no matter how good the manuscript proves itself to be, the writer responsible for the pitch has consigned its opening pages to being read under a cloud of confusion whilst the agent tries to figure out what type of book they've been sent.

By contrast, TITLE Y gives a real flavour of the book and is, therefore, more likely to grab the attention of an agent considering it. The pitch provides a genre, time period, setting and the central conflict. It also finishes with an intriguing question, inviting the reader into the narrative while hinting at things perhaps not being as straightforward for the protagonist as it might first appear. Finally, notice how without having read the book (and knowing relatively little about it) this pitch succeeds because, whether it's to your taste or not, you're able to place it.

## Is it unusual to find writing a pitch difficult?

Not at all. Distilling your book down to just a couple of sentences is a challenging task, and one agents know only too well given they need to make sure they're happy with (usually after discussing with their author) the way they articulate a book to those commissioning editors they're set to approach. Sometimes the best way to phrase the essence of a book can arrive straight away, while at other times the right words are hard to come by.

It's not the end of the world, then, if you're not entirely satisfied with the snappy description of your book you include in your covering letter. Your opening chapters are still likely to get read; it's understandable that being so heavily invested in a book can cloud your thinking. By sticking to the basics, though, you should be able to produce something that offers *enough*. An idea of the genre of your book, an idea of what type of book you've written as well as who and/ or what makes it tick. Or for non-fiction, the overall concept of your book and the headline things you're going to reveal to the reader. If you put your search for a perfect description to one side, you should be able to do this. Also, maybe go back to why you're submitting to the agent in the first place. Are they looking for a particular type of science fiction books? If that's what you've written, tell them – it's bound to be a good start in their eyes. Then tell them about your character and the dilemma they face (i.e. what do they stand to lose?). Next, does your book fall somewhere between other notable works of science fiction? (If so, mention them to give the agent some context.) All of a sudden you should have the basis of two or three sentences that encapsulate what your book is, and that get an agent in the right mindset to read your opening chapters.

One other useful way to approach writing a pitch for your book if you're struggling to get it right, is to seek some outside opinion. How would you describe your book to a friend in conversation? How would someone who's read your book describe it to you? This might be the sort of objective take you need.

## How do I know if my pitch is any good?

How do people react when you tell them what your book is about? Do they want to read it? Do they say it sounds interesting? It's all relative to their literary taste, of course, but gauging reaction to your description should leave you with a sense of whether you've got it right or not. And you shouldn't be short of practice as soon as you make it known that you're writing. It's inevitable that some people will ask 'What's it about, then?', so why not prepare for this moment? Rather than stumble through a rambling explanation that makes their eyes glaze over, use it as an opportunity to try out the lines you've been working on ahead of querying literary agents.

## How important is the title of my book?

Put some thought into your title ahead of submitting to an agent because it's important but ... don't be wedded to it because if your book goes on to be represented and then published, it could change several times. An agent may suggest alternatives, and its possible further suggestions could come from the team at your eventual publisher. This isn't guaranteed to happen, of course (everyone could agree you've got it spot on), and if it does then you'll have a say in the discussion, but you need to know that this process could happen (and a good example of your book no longer solely belonging to you).

Why do titles change? Because publishers appreciate they are major assets of the books they publish. In fact, a title arguably functions as the very first way in which an author pitches their book (either to an agent as part of the submission process, or to a reader looking at a bookshelf). Done well (and when published, coupled with all of the subliminal messages sent out by a striking cover design), it can heighten intrigue *and* present the core of a book. Think about some best-selling fiction titles of late: Paula Hawkins' *The Girl On The Train* (What about the girl on the train? What's she doing and where is she going?); David Nicholls' *One Day* (What happens on the day?); Gail Honeyman's *Eleanor Oliphant Is Completely Fine* (She can't be completely fine if the whole book is about her. What's *really* wrong with her?). And for non-fiction, how about Adam Kay's *This Is Going To Hurt* for a title that kick-starts curiosity?

## I've written my pitch but where should it appear in the covering letter?

It should appear towards the top of your covering letter. Your book is the reason you're writing to an agent, so don't bury it: tell them about it as soon as possible. Another reason why it's good to be succinct in a covering letter is that this allows your pitch a bit of space to breathe. Everything else (writing background, why you're writing to the agent, contact details) should all still be there, just not in the way of what your book is about and who it's for.

And as above, while your pitch is something to be included in your covering letter, remember it can travel well beyond this single-page document. It can be something you turn to when asked to explain your book to friends; it's the sort of catchy explainer an agent will use when in conversation with an editor, and if your book goes on to be published then a version could be used in selling the book. If it's good, it will go everywhere with your book.

## How do I pitch a book that's the first in a series?

An agent needs to know that your book is the first in a planned series, so do mention this prominently in your covering letter; maybe as a sentence that follows on from your book-specific pitch ('I see BOOK TITLE as the first in a five-part series featuring Detective NAME, whose unquenchable thirst for justice in London's corridors of power can only lead to one conclusion – he breaks the system, or the system breaks him.')

That said, if you do have a series of books in mind – either set in the same fantasy world or which introduces a recurring protagonist – then it's crucial not to get ahead of yourself when querying an agent. Stick to pitching the first in the series only. The fact that you've got more to come is definitely something of interest to an agent, but *only* if they like Book One. Your sole focus, therefore, must be about this book being watertight. If you have a series-long character arc plotted out, for example, then you have to come to terms with this being of interest only to you for the time being. Talking about the rest of the series in detail within your covering letter risks taking attention away from Book One, which is what you need to get published in order for the rest of the series to stand a chance of following suit.

# The covering letter: comparisons

Comparing your book to another piece of work can be a concise and impactful technique to employ when pitching to agents. A well-made comparison succeeds because it can combine features synonymous with other books (or TV or film) that can both catch an agent's attention and prepare them for the world they'll encounter in your opening chapters. It should give them the gist of what they're about to read stylistically and, with this established, allow them to assess how the writing does justice to the setting, tone and voice they might expect based on the comparison you've made.

Do exercise some caution around how you compare your book to other work, however. An ill-judged comparison could serve to undermine your writing if it doesn't meet an agent's expectations. Imagine buying a cinema ticket to watch the latest thriller and getting a French art-house film instead. No matter how good the art-house film actually proves to be, your initial confusion and disappointment is highly likely to cloud your judgement on first watch. Misfiring manuscript comparisons work in the same way and, assuming you've got a very limited amount of an agent's time, could lead to an underwhelming first impression of your work from which it might not recover. Have you compared your book to two other pieces of work that have absolutely no common ground? Or, perhaps more dangerously, have you suggested your book is on par with a best-selling book or award-winning author? This could be an innocent mistake brought about by semantics, but it's your job as an author to be aware of the consequences. There's a big difference between saying you're 'the next JK Rowling' and suggesting your book 'could appeal to fans of *Harry Potter*', for example, with the latter a much more humble, target market-specific, and realistic stance.

Essentially, before using a comparison to help 'place' your work, consider this simple question: does your writing back it up? If so, it's a good tool to have at your disposal. And finally, although your book as a whole might bear the hallmarks of a particular book, film or TV series, if you're going to make mention of this in your covering letter, then you have to actually bear this out in the opening chapters you submit (which doesn't necessarily mean a huge set-piece, but there should be stylistic leanings in terms of the language chosen and the way your plot begins to unfold).

## What if a comparison doesn't spring to mind?

Don't overreach for one because it'll be obvious if you're doing so. While a comparison is great if you can find one that works for your book, it's far from a requirement of a covering letter, so if you don't feel confident in using one, just leave it out. It could even be that one becomes attached to your book at the suggestion of your agent or publisher at a later date.

If you are finding it difficult to draw comparisons between your book and other 'touchstone' works, however, ask yourself whether you're reading enough. The only way to comfortably assess where your book fits in to the market, and what it does differently, is to be a reader and general consumer of all things linked to what your book is about. But this shouldn't be limited to 'heritage' authors or genre-defining books. While these may obviously prove influential, when submitting your manuscript you need to be reading the work of debut authors too. These are relevant to your situation in two ways: they're the books publishers are buying right now; and their authors are therefore represented by agents working in your part of the market that might be interested in your book. If you're about to start researching agents, this is as good a place to begin as any.

SEE ALSO *What if my book is impossible to categorise?* page 41.

## Should I compare my writing style to that of another author?

If you think it works, then do it: it's a great easy-access point to the sort of narrative you've looked to create. Again though, just be careful about stitching yourself up by how you put this across. For example, if you think your book gives a nod to the pace of Martina Cole but has also been infused by your love of Ann Patchett, and – crucially – a sense of this comes across within your opening pages, this would be a wonderful way to summarise to an agent the blend of writing they can expect. However, don't include a bald statement such as 'I write like Ann Patchett' and 'My writing's as good as Martina Cole's' because this sort of attitude is going to make an agent bristle.

Linked to the example above, another thing to consider when comparing your work to other authors (or particular titles) is whether or not you need to refer to a heavyweight author. True, claiming your crime novel 'feels somewhere between John Le Carré and Agatha Christie' is an attention-grabbing statement to make, but is it *actually* going to be on par with either body of work? And looking at the current marketplace, would it go on to sell? The agent you're submitting to will definitely know of all the contemporary authors writing in your part of the market, so might it be more effective to compare your work to someone more recent?

Also, what's to say you can't be a little more specific in any comparison you make? Why not choose a particular trait an author is known for in order to give a sense of your book without flirting with the danger of a direct comparison? This 'Style X meets Style Y' technique can work particularly well for writers of a cross-genre book, and may also make an agent think: 'I wonder how that's going to work?'

Finally, a simple solution not to lose sight of is to say your work is 'influenced' by a certain author. So long as this is justified within your writing sample then this seems a safer way to draw comparison to the work of other writers.

SEE ALSO *The covering letter: examples and exercises* page 125.

## Can I compare my book to a film or TV show?

Provided the genre and tone of the comparisons you're drawing are a good fit for your manuscript, then absolutely. It's probably better to give at least one nod to a genre-sensitive book or author to show that you're a keen reader in your part of the market, but mixing that up with a nod to a TV series or film could be helpful. Remember, the purpose of using comparison as a device is purely to help give an agent a flavour of what to expect from your writing, and if there's something suitable outside of the world of books that does this then it makes complete sense to use it to your advantage.

## How do I compare my work to something else and make it sound 'fresh'?

If you're writing genre fiction, you might be concerned about your work echoing story arcs that have gone before. Your challenge as a writer, therefore, is to either do something different within this structure, or adjust it slightly. Can you find a style or voice or setting or character that makes an agent lean forward in their chair? This is about finding something 'fresh' – a story that does something to shake itself free from the type of manuscript an agent has been used to reading for the last couple of years.

And drawing comparison to something that's been published before doesn't prevent you from pitching a book that's 'innovative'. How about Ben Aaronovitch's *Rivers of London*, which was pitched as

'Harry Potter meets Raymond Chandler' and offers a fresh take on the idea of a detective story. Or Stuart Turton's *The Seven Deaths of Evelyn Hardcastle*, which was billed as 'like an Agatha Christie novel meets *Groundhog Day*'.

Yes, both examples take the risk of drawing comparison to hugely successful authors or projects, but because each statement helps readers understand what they're getting – and then the books go on to deliver – it doesn't matter. First the reader asks 'How is the author going to pull it off?' and next, upon realising the comparison is entirely justified, they think 'It's so exciting to read something new'.

## I'm writing non-fiction. Should I compare my book to market competitors?

Yes. It's the sort of information an agent needs in a proposal. Even if you can't offer sales figures (something your agent will help with before sending out a proposal to editors) it's still good to mention the other books you're going up against because:

- it shows you have a good understanding of the current market;
- and it also provides the perfect opportunity to say what your book does better or differently to those already available to buy.

Comparisons made within a non-fiction proposal can be more pointed (rather than the less clinical 'My book is in the same sort of style as' or 'it will appeal to readers of' approach a fiction author might take). Has another book sold particularly well in the same subject area as you? Does your book offer a different take? Is the book you've written tapping into a particular trend? And if this trend is an emerging one, how are you going to prove there's an audience ready to buy your book?

Directly comparing your book to others in the same field is also useful in viewing your work in context, and what you believe is its USP (unique selling point). This is exactly what agents want to know and they'll probably work with you to make more of this ahead of sending your proposal to publishers because it could be considered a readymade marketing and publicity angle to help gain support in an acquisitions meeting.

# The covering letter: examples and exercises

## Pitching within your covering letter

Being successful in gaining the representation of a literary agent is all about the book … but a well-crafted pitch is definitely a useful tool to have at your disposal. Not only can it help to initially attract the attention of an agent within your covering letter, it can be used at every step of a book's journey thereafter: from a commissioning editor making its case in an acquisitions meeting to a bookseller using it to sell a copy to a customer. Here are some useful exercises to consider as you attempt to hone your pitch for inclusion in your covering letter:

- step away from the manuscript. Coming back to something and re-reading with a fresh pair of eyes is always recommended by published writers, so why not follow their logic and, at the point of trying to find the right words to encapsulate your work, give yourself some distance from it? The story will continue to ruminate and chances are, mid-way through your commute or doing the washing up, the right words will appear …

- use 'What if'. If your book centres around a concept that basically asks this question, why not use it to your advantage and lead with it?

- ask a trusted reader to summarise your book for you. Why not ask more than one to see if there are any similarities to the words they use? This could prove useful when trying to unlock that magic turn of phrase you feel is missing;

- study the blurbs on the backs of books lining your shelves at home. Choose ones in your genre that have influenced you, or you feel close to stylistically. Can you write something like this but in a couple of sentences (with your genre, word count and any comparisons made around this)?

- use a particularly good line in your book to open your covering letter. (It does *need* to be good if you're going to do this.) Could it work as a standalone introduction to what your book is about and, say, the dilemma your protagonist faces? You'd be expected to include genre, word count and comparisons afterwards but this could be an impactful way to present a lead character with a distinctive voice;

- if you're struggling to distil your book down to just a few sentences, set the ball rolling by allowing yourself to write a paragraph. Check whether everything you've written is specific to your main character and how the plot moves forward. Now see if you can condense it to three sentences. And then have a look at shaving it down to one or two sentences. It's not necessarily an easy thing to do, but it is a good exercise in making you recognise what's really at the core of your manuscript.

## Covering letter examples

A quick disclaimer: neither of the following letters entirely fit their description. The successful letter isn't perfect, while the unsuccessful example isn't *all* bad. What's clear, however, is one has been written by a writer who's taken a considered, professional approach to introducing their book, while the other has come from someone taking a punt, not fully committed to their craft and almost hoping for an agent to do them a favour by investing a bit of faith. Moving personal literary tastes to one side for a moment, a simple question: as first impressions go, which writer would you prefer to work with?

Both letters, however, are legible and give at least the gist of what the manuscript they accompany is about. As a result, most agents would probably turn to their opening pages to read some of the work. Yet for the writer of the unsuccessful letter, this is only likely to amount to a cursory glance. Their covering letter has served to lower expectations of the quality of their work, with an agent turning to page 1 as a means of nothing more than due diligence. There's always the chance that the writing is a bit better than what's contained within the covering letter, but they've read enough half-baked submissions before to know not to hold their breath.

The 'successful' letter places an agent in a completely different mindset. After reading this, an agent will open the first pages of the manuscript optimistically, ready to give the book serious consideration because it obviously belongs to a writer who's approaching the idea of being published seriously. They've bothered to research and personalise their submission, and also set the book up with a concise pitch. In short, their letter has not only given their book a chance, it's succeeded in making the agent want to put time aside for it without them even having read the first sentence. Which is exactly what a covering letter really needs to do.

### UNSUCCESSFUL COVERING LETTER

This letter has been deliberately designed as a realistic but flawed approach for representation. As a result, it's coherent, relatively concise, has a structure, and the writer does make an attempt to say what the book is. Up to a point, then, it's just about done its job. Yet rather than any specific mistake the writer is guilty of (and there are many) it's perhaps their approach in general that's most problematic. Before an agent turns to the manuscript itself, the lack of research or professionalism of any kind (as well as complete failure to create any sort of excitement or buzz around the book) means the writer has undermined their work. Even if their first three chapters go on to be better than the quality of the letter suggests, can they do enough to make an agent – who, subliminally, has begun wondering whether this is a writer worth their time, effort and expertise – change their mind?

**(1)** Dear Sir/Madam,

**(2)** Like the other agents I've already sent this to, I'm sure you're unlikely to be **(3)** interested but ... I thought I owed it to myself to send you an email anyway!

I'm looking for a literary agent and, because I admire the authors you represent, **(4)**
**(5)** I wondered weather you might like to take a look at the first draft of my **(6)**
**(7)** fictional novel, TITLE, which every fan of thrillers is going to buy! My **(8)**
**(9)** friends love it and say they've never read anything like it before so fingers **(10)**
crossed you feel the same way!

As you'll be able to see, my style is a bit like Haruki Murakami, Cormac **(11)**
McCarthy and Hilary Mantel mixed together. I think this book has a chance of
selling more copies than them, though. To give you the best taster of TITLE
(which should end up at around 50,000 words when I get back from travelling) **(12)**
**(13)** I thought I'd attach chapters 5, 8 and 12 because they're better than the first
**(14)** three. I've had to attach a five-page synopsis as well because there are so
many twists and turns in the story.

**(15)** TITLE © follows the emotional journey of a lost orphaned boy and the troubles **(16)**
he must overcome not just to survive … but to find himself. This is the first
fictional novel I have written but I'm quite prolific and have been working on **(17)**
**(18)** another project (a fantasy book for children) for the last few months. I should
complete this by the end of the year and then I'll return to one of the other ideas
I have for further fictional novels – I have dozens!

I'm happy to work with an editor to make the book tighter, but hope you enjoy it **(19)**
as it is, and that you want to read more when it's finished.

**(20)** I have written all of my life and really hope you would like to help me fulfil the
dream of seeing my stories available in stores throughout the UK. You'll see **(21)**
I've also attached one other file to show you how serious I am about this book.
My best friend is a professional graphic designer, and I commissioned him to **(22)**
work on the cover, which he is hoping will appear on the published version so
he can earn some money from the book being published too.

Thanks in advance for your time. If I don't hear back from you within two **(23)**
working weeks then I'll be sure to follow up by email.

**(24)** A.N Author xx

**Unsuccessful covering letter**

The numbered points below relate to the letter opposite.

1. Failing to address the recipient by their name immediately makes the letter feel like a copy-and-paste job. Already the agent is starting to question whether the material they're about to read is *actually* going to be something they're interested in. How would you feel if they replied to your request for representation with a letter that began with 'Dear Writer'? Beginning a letter in this way also makes agents question the amount of research the writer has done before sending their work. A 'general' agent doesn't exist; you need one with an understanding and passion for your book, and for your career as an author.

2. Quite passive aggressive in tone, and seems like it's from a writer who has become despondent, frustrated and cynical about the process. It's much better to be positive about the book and what you have to offer as an author.

3. Why should the agent bother, then? It sounds as though many of their peers have already rejected the book, so why should they feel differently? The author has fallen into the trap of being self-deprecating, and apologetic about their work. 'Imposter syndrome' is dangerous because it can give the impression you're not taking your work seriously. If you think your book is good enough, then back yourself and be confident, especially in front of an industry professional.

4. Nice to include but not specific. A lack of examples reinforces the suspicion that the letter hasn't been written to the individual agent.

5. Spelling mistakes can happen to everyone but if two or three appear then an agent will wonder if the writer *really* cares about their work. Are they going to be someone who needs a huge amount of editorial assistance to reach the standard of writing required?

6. Never send out a first draft of anything. It will never be as good as a re-worked, closely edited version of a manuscript. Agents operate on the basis that you're sending them the best you can do, so it's a huge risk to send out a first draft.

7. A mistake made more frequently than you'd think!

8. Placing the book with a target audience is a good thing to do but to claim *everyone* is going to buy it is unrealistic. At best this is naivety, at worst it's a show of arrogance.

9. Are friends and/or family the best barometer for feedback? Are they widely read in your genre, and will they give objective, constructive criticism?

10. It's lazy, unrealistic and/or arrogant to state your book is totally original. It's also very unlikely to be true. If it is *genuinely* original, however, then two thoughts spring to mind: you should either be incredibly excited to be adding to the literary canon; or there's a good reason why a book like yours hasn't been published.

11. Comparisons can be a useful tool but do the writer more harm than good here. Are these authors of crime/thriller novels? What does a book that brings together the writing styles of these authors even begin to look like? If we don't know, the comparison has failed. Also, the writer suggests their book is destined to sell as many books as these authors. It's naive or arrogant to expect as much.

12. 50,000 words feels quite short for a manuscript written for readers of this genre. A greater concern, though, is that the author doesn't seem to have finished the book. Consider this a must if you're writing fiction.

13. All agents ask for the opening chapters of your book because they want to read it exactly as a reader would. If your book doesn't engage the agent beyond the first fifty pages then, like the average book-buyer, they'll give up on it.

14. If you've written an incredibly long, complex piece of crime fiction, you could perhaps get away with your synopsis being *slightly* over the page count requested. To go this much over, though, makes an agent think you don't have a handle on your plot.

15. Is it really necessary to protect your work before sending it to an agent? Is it really worthwhile for them to risk their reputation by stealing something that you can prove to be your intellectual property?

16. There are two things wrong with this pitch. It arrives too late in the letter, and it feels completely generic. It's interesting that the boy has been orphaned, but who is he? What's his name? How old is he? How was he orphaned and when? Where is the story set? What does he need to overcome? What are the dangers he needs to survive? Specificity is key to a good pitch and this sentence contains none.

17. Self-aggrandising and genuinely an unremarkable thing to say. The very least an agent expects of any author they work with is that they're hard-working.

18. This brings up two issues. First, does the agent reading this letter also represent YA fantasy fiction? If not, this information is going to put them off. Second, the next book *not* being in the crime/thriller genre could be a concern. Should building readers in the same part of the market come first?

19. The writer appears open to editorial work, which is good, but there's a question mark here against why they didn't make sure the manuscript was in the best shape possible before submitting it. Why should the agent bother with them if they can't be bothered to finish something to the standard expected?

20. Another unremarkable statement. Unless you have genuine writing credentials or need to include information that gives your manuscript greater authenticity, it's probably better not to include anything at all regarding your writing background.

21. Only the UK? Would it not appeal to readers in other countries? It's fine if that's the case, but if a book has a chance of selling to publishers operating in other territories, it's a more attractive proposition.

22. This is an unnecessary thing to have done because part of a publisher's job is to commission someone to work on cover design, and they are extremely unlikely to use the designs you have already paid for.

23. Don't be pushy. An agent's submission guidelines state how long a writer should expect to wait for a response to their request for representation. Only after that time has elapsed is it reasonable to send a polite chaser email.

24. Striking a balance of personable and professional can sometimes prove difficult, but this is definitely too informal. Would you sign off a job application with kisses?

SUCCESSFUL COVERING LETTER

As mentioned above, the fact this is classed as a successful letter is not to preach perfection or claim to be the only letter template writers should use. The number of variables at play for each author approaching an agent (the type of book they're submitting and how they articulate this; relevant background information; previous writing experience; things that have inspired the book, particular reasons behind choosing to submit to the agent) points towards the most effective approach being a bespoke one.

What should be clear is this letter is succinct and professional yet personable in tone. It's from a writer serious about their craft; who knows what their book is and who's likely to want to read it. All of these things amount to credit in the bank with the agent they're asking to put time aside for their writing. Assuming they're intrigued by the book's concept and/or protagonist and the writing's good, then taking into account the professional approach shown by the writer displayed within the covering letter ... all of a sudden this is a submission – and a writer – they want to know more about.

From: a.n.author@gmail.com

Subject: [Title] by [Author Name]

(1) Dear [AGENT NAME],

I am writing to seek representation for my fantasy fiction novel, TITLE, which (2) is for young adult readers and 75,000 words in length. I wanted to send it to (3) you as I'm a big fan of [AUTHOR X], who I understand you represent.

(4) TITLE is the story of Anna Molly, an impatient 15-year-old who, along with Aristotle (her black cat), have been relocated to a corner of the coastal town of Dungeness. Unfortunately for Anna, trouble is never far behind: unexplained black circles begin appearing over every house in the town, with deadly symptoms reported by her neighbours. The world's media can only gawp as Anna, with little to lose and absolutely no intention of living the rest of her life under a cloud, steps onto her roof and towards a world even darker than the one she is about to leave behind.

I see TITLE as a standalone work pitched somewhere between Neil Gaiman's (5) *The Ocean at the End of the Lane* and Netflix's *Stranger Things*, and feel it will (6) have a strong appeal to an audience aged 14 years and above.

(7) Since completing a Creative Writing course at Goldsmiths, where I began working on TITLE, I have also written a number of short stories and am making (8) good progress with a new fantasy novel more in the style of Margo Lanagan. (9)(10) I live with my partner in York, and work as a teacher.

I hope you enjoy TITLE and look forward to hearing from you soon.

Regards,

A.N Author

(11) [EMAIL ADDRESS]
[07872 xxx xxx]
[@TwitterHandle]

**Successful covering letter**

The numbered points below relate to the letter on the previous page.

1.  By addressing the agent by name, the writer is immediately going to elicit more of a response: 'They must have looked me up, be aware of the sort of books I represent, and therefore pitching something that's likely to interest me.'

2.  Book title, target audience and word length all dealt with succinctly.

3.  Reaffirms to the agent the writer has done their research and written to them specifically. They're serious about their book, making the agent want to invest their time in considering it carefully.

4.  This paragraph tells us all we need to know to get to grips with the story: the name of the protagonist, her age, call to adventure, and the real-world to fantasy-world set up. Whether you like the idea or not, you now know what's at the heart of the book.

5.  The contemporary literary and TV comparisons used here complement each other and are used to good effect. The author doesn't give the impression they believe their work is destined to mirror their success; they use them as cultural touchstones, however, to heighten interest and give a better idea of the tone of their book.

6.  Further evidence of the writer having a real knowledge of their corner of the market. They've mentioned genre above, but now they're specifying by a particular age group. Also, this age works well with the age of their protagonist, whose relatability is a key aspect of a story appealing to a particular age group of reader.

7.  Writing qualifications and/or experience relevant to the book are always worth including if you have something to say. This doesn't need to be a formal course; working on a checkout for twenty years could be just as interesting provided it's in some way related to the book you're submitting.

8. It's good to know that there's more to come, and most agents don't mind you including a one-line pitch for the second book if you have one ready ...

9. ... particularly if the next book is going to be of interest to the same sort of audience as the first. Again, the writer refers to another author in the genre, reinforcing they're someone who knows and understands what they're trying to achieve in their writing.

10. This tiny snapshot of the author's life gives a sense of what they might be like as a person.

11. It's always worthwhile leaving your contact details at the end of your covering letter. Some agents may want to speak to you over the phone, while others might find it useful to have your email address to hand because of the way they process their submissions. In quite an understated way, the writer has also decided to include a link to a social media profile, suggesting it's something they're comfortable with.

# The synopsis

The synopsis is an important document because it lays a manuscript bare. There's no place for structure to hide or room for your main character to go missing; the sentences that make up this document are the spine of your book and are judged as such by an agent assessing your work. The challenge is simple: in a matter-of-fact way, are you able to commit the major plot-points of your book to no more than one side of A4?

Writers of fiction and narrative non-fiction can find the synopsis a frustrating document to write because it requires them to boil their book down to the bare bones. It doesn't matter about prose or emotion or nuance, just the information that drives the narrative forward. This can force a writer to face up to flaws in their manuscript, particularly from a structural point of view. And it's for this reason that a synopsis is required by those behind the scenes working on the book; namely the writer, their agent (who will offer editorial assistance ahead of the manuscript going out on submission) and the publishing house editor. The synopsis becomes a point of reference for all involved, enabling a helicopter view of a manuscript to make sure the story works as a complete piece and not just on a sentence by sentence, paragraph by paragraph basis.

From the point of view of an agent at the stage of reading an unsolicited manuscript submission, the synopsis provides assurance. Assurance that the writer has written the full manuscript. Assurance that the writer understands what makes a manuscript tick through to the end. And assurance at being able to see how the book as a whole pans out before taking the decision to ask to read the manuscript in full.

Yet this shouldn't lead you to overestimate where the synopsis sits in the pecking order of submission documents. No book will ever be signed on the strength of a synopsis alone, and nor will one be turned down if it's a bit flabby. In reading through your submission, the first thing an agent will look at is your covering letter. And then at this point, most agents tend to differ with what they do next: some will turn to your opening chapters, while others will skim through your synopsis to get an idea of where your book is leading. Either way, though, the synopsis is unlikely to be given serious consideration unless an agent is intrigued and impressed by the opening pages of your manuscript.

## What is a synopsis?

It's a quick-view document of the book as a whole for people behind the scenes (author, agent, editor), and therefore not one that readers will see. Most agency guidelines ask for it to be submitted alongside a covering letter and the opening section of your book, and for it to be no longer than a single page. The synopsis should be a straightforward reporting of the main events of your book, presenting the journey of the protagonist(s) in the order in which it unfolds for the reader. It should therefore include the beginning, middle and end of your book, and include the Who, What, Where and When of a story (but not necessarily the Why and the How).

An agent is likely to assess your synopsis in closer detail as part of deciding whether or not to ask to read your full manuscript. If they make you an offer of representation and you accept, your synopsis may be looked at and changed in accordance with any structural work your manuscript undergoes. A revised version of your synopsis will accompany an agent's submission of your work to prospective commissioning editors.

## Why is a synopsis necessary?

Because it's a user manual for your book. If there's a plot hole, it will become evident; if a character arc needs reconsidering, it can help point to where and why; and if a scene needs moving, it provides an idea of the knock-on effect this could have on the shape of the rest of your book.

As a result, some writers don't necessarily wait until they officially need to produce a synopsis as part of their manuscript submission. If you're a writer who hasn't considered this, why not put some time aside to write one (not necessarily to fit a single side of A4) after completing a first draft? Could this straightforward retelling of the events of your book prove useful in honing your story, and make key scenes as impactful as they should be? It stands to reason that having a bird's-eye view of your story – and not just a fixation on the ebb and flow of sentences and paragraphs – can provide a writer with invaluable context as they develop their work.

Agents ask for a synopsis because they want to zoom out and see how your book as a whole shapes up. It's great if your opening chapters grab an agent's interest, but the next question they have is whether you've only written a brilliant opening, or you have a strong understanding of the entire book? Do you have the know-how to guide a reader through the middle section of a book and keep them engaged? And does your ending actually deliver? Is it as powerful as it should be? A synopsis helps an agent ask these questions of writers. It gives them something to point to outside of the manuscript itself.

Another reason agents ask to see a synopsis is one steeped in pragmatism: their time is at a premium, so they don't want to waste it on reading a full manuscript that, for example, has an absurd ending. Before requesting a full manuscript, an agent will assess the synopsis quite carefully to make sure this isn't the case. Basically, they need to know the book isn't (to the misfortune of the writer affected) very similar to something else one of their clients is already working on, and that there's a logic to how the narrative progresses. Manuscripts will not be turned down if an agent spots a slight flaw in the way things pan out, nor if there's a difference of opinion about how it ends. Synopses containing sections with an obvious lack of definition or which take a completely inexplicable turn, however, are likely to put an agent off contacting the writer. These sorts of flaws tend to be a warning sign for a writer either not knowing their book well enough or having not actually finished it.

## Why am I finding it hard to write a synopsis?

First, don't think of the synopsis as being reductive of your story. See it as simply telling it in a different way. Condensing upwards of 70,000 to just a single side of A4, however, is understandably a task that can flummox writers, and may require a bit more time to get right than one expects. Here are some potential reasons behind a struggle to write a synopsis:

- **it's a different type of writing.** Given that most agency guidelines ask for the synopsis to be no more than a single page, writing in a more matter-of-fact way can be quite difficult for writers to get to grips with, especially after working on their own terms and being immersed in the world of their manuscript for so long;

- **just state what happens.** Part of this shift in writing style can be fuelled by a writer's reluctance to purely include the main beats of a plot. Don't succumb to the temptation of mentioning perfectly crafted moments between secondary characters if they don't progress the main story you're telling. Don't include description or the reason why something matters, either; let your plot do all the talking for you;

- **your book might not be tight enough.** All a synopsis demands is that you retell the events of your plot. If this doesn't prove as easy to fashion as you might have hoped, it probably means there are kinks in the narrative to be ironed out, and some rewriting needs to be done. In this case, the synopsis is doing the same job for the writer as it does for the agent. If written correctly, it should provide a completely objective view of a narrative; one that doesn't pander to a writer's feelings but serves the story they have written.

# Does it matter if my synopsis is too long?

How long is too long? Always check agency guidelines ahead of sending and then do your absolute best to adhere to what they say. Yes, most ask for a single side of A4, but some say two pages while others give you a word count to work with.

To be able to put your story across as concisely as possible tends to indicate you're a writer who is completely sure of their story and that it's tightly structured. However, if your synopsis exceeds the word or page count required by hundreds of words, chances are you need to either put some more work into being succinct; your narrative might not be tight enough to allow what's at the heart of your book to really resonate.

As with the covering letter, though, if you find your synopsis creeps onto a second page by just a paragraph, in all probability that won't be the reason why an agent passes up the opportunity to offer representation. As a result, then, so long as it's as tight as you can make it and as close to the guidelines as possible, just send it. It's unlikely to be a deal-breaker.

A synopsis should be … :

- **straightforward.** There is no expectation for a synopsis to be anything beyond a technical document that maps out what drives your manuscript forward. Don't make a rod for your own back by writing from the perspective of your protagonist or by replicating the style of your narrative. Just retell your story in the order it's relayed to the reader;

- **revealing.** A synopsis summarise what happens in your story in simple sentences. Any character details should be brief and limited to those that are major players in the narrative. Details about your novel's setting should appear, but are not as important as key *events* in your story;

- **easy to follow.** The plot should unfold in exactly the way it does in the book itself. Upon mentioning a main character for the first time, write their name in CAPS.

Note that writers of non-narrative non-fiction are generally asked to provide a more detailed chapter outline as an accompanying document to their manuscript.

A synopsis should not ... :

- **include cliff-hangers.** A synopsis is a nuts-and-bolts reference tool for those who get a say on the shape of the story (writer, agent and editor), so don't worry about spoilers. All of these people need to be on the inside track because they want to assess how your narrative has been put together and work with you to make sure you achieve maximum impact from every scene written and character created;

- **be flabby.** Stick as closely as possible to the agency submission guidelines that apply to each agent you query. As noted several times previously, if they ask for a one-page synopsis, then do your absolute best to meet that criteria. Don't complicate things by introducing secondary characters or background information: just report the main events that progress your plot;

- **contain the *why* and the *how*.** Concentrate on including the Who, What, Where and When but not necessarily the Why and the How. If your plot and character arcs make sense, then they'll speak for themselves.

## What's the difference between a blurb and a synopsis?

A blurb appears on the back of a book cover or jacket and its purpose is to sell your story. It's there to give a sense of what the book is and leave prospective readers wondering where the narrative is going to take them. The synopsis is a totally separate, fuss-free piece of writing that directs the reader from beginning to middle to end. It reports the main events of a narrative and is used solely as a behind-the-scenes reference tool by the writer, their agent and their publisher.

## Should my synopsis include the ending of my book?

The majority of agents want you to include your ending in the synopsis.

It's understandable for some to want more of a 'reader's-eye' experience of a manuscript upon reading for the first time (therefore taking the decision *not* to look at the end of the synopsis) but more generally, the expectation from an agent is that the document will tell them all they need to know about how your narrative moves forward. An agent's job is to interrogate the structure and character arcs of your story to make sure the most is being wrung from every scene you write. In order to achieve a more powerful ending, should a scene at the beginning be rewritten or removed altogether, for example? And how about pacing? Are there moments in the manuscript laden by exposition that could be avoided by adding in another plot point? Without being able to see the full picture (i.e. how a story resolves), it's impossible for them to judge. (If you are determined, however, to have your ending remain a surprise, then your synopsis must end with the final choice presented to your protagonist without revealing what they decide to do.)

## How do I introduce a series in a synopsis?

There's no exact science to this but it seems logical to mention this at either the very beginning of your synopsis, or at the very end. This should be no more than a couple of lines, though (i.e. not an excuse to produce a much longer document than requested), because the primary focus of your submission needs to be the *first* book. Too much detail about sequel titles risks over-complicating things and drawing attention away from Book One, which holds the key to any related work that follows being published.

Books classed as 'series' tend to fall into two categories: interlinked books that progress an overarching narrative; or a standalone book with a character an author wants to base further titles around. Using *Lord of the Rings* as an example for the former, a synopsis for *The Fellowship of the Ring* (in which the quest to destroy the One Ring is set up but remains unfulfilled by the time the book ends) would be completely misshapen and confusing without mention of the journey being set to continue in the next book. Similarly, writing a standalone book that introduces a protagonist you'd like to base more books around is a useful detail to add, particularly if your manuscript devotes more time to their back story as a result, and there are certain elements of their character arc that are not quite tied up.

---

**Exercises:** Here are a couple of prompts that might prove useful if you're struggling to get to grips with writing a synopsis.

- Ask someone who has *not* read your book to read and comment on your synopsis. Does the story make sense to them? Assuming your synopsis is a straightforward retelling of the key events of your narrative, the questions they raise will either mean you need to tweak your synopsis to make something clearer, or they may have identified a genuine flaw in your plot that needs addressing.

- Conversely, could you run a version of your synopsis past someone who *has* read your book? Do they think it's a good assessment of the nuts and bolts of your plot? And/or have you failed to include something they found essential to making the plot plausible?

- Finally, if you're struggling to adapt to the style needed to write a synopsis, why not take the pressure off by scrutinising something else for a while? Try writing a synopsis for a favourite book, or relax into a film and then, as soon as it's finished, try to produce a one-pager that describes the story.

## I'm writing short-form fiction. Is a synopsis required?

Submission guidelines obviously differ from agency to agency, but if you're writing any form of prose fiction then expect to have to provide a synopsis alongside your manuscript.

If you're writing text for children's picture books, you're unlikely to be asked for one, and the agent will just be happy with a sentence describing what the book is about within your covering letter (this would basically double as your pitch). This could be slightly longer if you're introducing a character you plan to base a number of books around (very popular with younger children – from *Mog* through to *Peter Rabbit*). Again, this wouldn't need to be a separate document and could appear in your covering letter. If you decide to submit more than one picture book to the agent, be sure to include a short explanation of what happens in each book (Character X goes to the zoo/Character X gets lost in the supermarket).

If you're seeking representation as a short story writer or poet then, again, check the agency submission guidelines carefully to be sure what's required. If you're asked to submit a single story/poem for consideration only, it's likely your synopsis wouldn't be expected to exceed more than a couple of lines (although do mention any common themes that link a wider collection together) and therefore can be included within the covering letter. If you're submitting an anthology of work, a document providing a plot summary per story seems a reasonable approach, but always double-check the agency website for guidance.

## What is a chapter outline?

This is a key part of a proposal for most non-fiction projects outside of memoir, and is generally expected to be five pages in length.

As its name suggests, a chapter outline should include a run-through of what's going to be covered within each chapter of a book, and leave an agent with a clear roadmap of how the entire manuscript is going to play out from beginning to end. It should be written clearly and concisely, with key information relayed in the same order as it appears in the manuscript (without statistics, data and/or graphs unless they are the absolute focus of a chapter).

Where a chapter outline differs from a synopsis is that it's expected to offer more detail on a chapter by chapter basis (making it a longer document overall), and its contents may hold greater sway over an agent's decision to offer an author representation or not.

The primary reason more detail is asked for in a chapter outline comes back to agents seeking assurance. Where non-narrative popular non-fiction titles are concerned, agents know readers question the information they're being presented with: who is this person to be telling me this? Why should I read what they think? These questions might feel crude, but they are being asked because author authenticity matters. Is the author a leader in their field or do they have a unique take on a particular subject? Without this sort of credibility, a book can be undermined from the outset and may face even more of an uphill battle for sales. A chapter outline allows an agent to get more of a grasp of how an author fares against this criteria without even having looked at a writing sample, and why (arguably) it's initially scrutinised by agents more than a synopsis for a work of fiction.

# The opening chapters

For fiction authors in particular, the challenge of getting an agent is never more real than when attaching the opening chapters of their manuscript. These are far and away the most important documents within your submission package, and should bring to the fore two elements of submissions to agents that are absolutely vital to gaining representation: submit only to agents who are interested in writing in a similar vein to your own; and when you do submit to those agents, such is the amount of competition you face from other unpublished writers vying for their attention, you need those opening chapters to sing.

Yes, there's every chance your submission is better than a lot of the others read by an agent that day, but if you're to convince an agent to invest their time and expertise into representing you and your work, you need to impress them on a whole new level. Very broadly put, agents are readers, and like any other reader they have a lot of other things going on that are demanding their time. So your writing has to be a lot more than competent or a decent reimagining of something that's been done time and time again; to get an offer of representation, you have to produce something that takes hold of an agent by their collar and pulls them towards your writing, forcing everything else to wait. Have you produced something that's a little bit different and that can hold its own amidst the competition? If so, do your opening chapters give a sense of this? In introducing your book, do they also encapsulate everything your book is going to be and make an agent want to read on? As agents look through the sample of writing you have approached them with, the reader and business sides of their brain will subconsciously begin to mull over the following sorts of questions:

- do I love it enough to want to read more?
- is it better than – or does it have enough of an edge over – other books in the same part of the market?

- do I know of any editors who would be interested in buying this sort of book?

There's no cynicism to be found in these questions, though. Agents *want* to find new writers with great ideas and fresh voices. As a result, if you're sure to submit to an agent interested in representing books similar to the one you've produced, you can almost guarantee they will begin reading your opening chapters as one of the most engaged readers you'll ever have. It's easy to think of agents as naysayers because of all of the tales of rejection you hear from other authors, but their default attitude towards a manuscript submission is actually very positive. They're an expert in the corner of the publishing marketplace you're writing in, and they genuinely hope your work is going to be something they enjoy and they'll be pleased you've chosen to submit to them. As a result, they click on a submission with a 'Yes' mindset and this remains the case until the writing, the concept, the market demand or the feeling of 'it's just not for me' counts a book out of the reckoning.

So, what do your opening chapters need to do? They have to engage an agent's attention and have something about them – the voice of your narrator, a protagonist that demands attention or general intrigue in the concept of your book – that keeps an agent saying 'Yes' to more.

## Why do agents only ask for the opening three chapters?

Because that's where a reader is going to start and, first and foremost, that's what an agent is (and a particularly avid reader of your type of book). The most logical way they can assess whether or not your writing works for them therefore has to be the book's opening, with the basic question being asked in the background as they turn the pages: 'Do I want to read on?' (If your book isn't set out in chapters, double-check your target agencies' maximum word count, and work to that instead.)

As a writer, one potentially tricky aspect of conforming to the requirements of submitting the opening of a book is making sure this section of writing showcases what's at its heart. You need to introduce your protagonist, the setting, your narrative voice alongside the central tension or concept that drives the book forward. These expectations apply to writers of memoir or biography as well. Can you establish an authorial voice and hook the reader into the story? Acknowledging the need to do this is key, and if you're not satisfied that your opening chapters do this effectively, you'd be wise to revisit them. For example, have you started your book in the right place? And does your narrative move forward at the pace it should?

Finally, for context, it's also worth appreciating how a request for the opening three chapters (or first 10,000 words) is actually a reasonable arrangement in a practical sense for both writers and agents. For writers, it helps create a level playing field; everyone is judged on the same number of words. And for agents, a word limit is a godsend. Not only is 10,0000 words/three chapters enough of a sample section to get an idea of whether they'd like to invest more time in working with an author, but some agents receive an average of between fifty and 100 submissions per week so a word limit is essential.

SEE ALSO *Do agents read everything a writer sends them?* page 155.

## Why do I need to have finished the whole manuscript if an agent's only going to read the first three chapters?

For two reasons. First, there's a difference between a good writer and a good writer *of books*. Beautiful prose is one thing, but a well-balanced full manuscript requires you to be able to keep your reader turning pages from the beginning through to the end. You can't hope to do this without the correct pace, and by choosing to reveal information to the reader at the right time. You can't hope to achieve any of *that* without having written the ending. Only when you can see the whole thing are you able to chisel away at the ordering of scenes, improve character arcs and more to create a structurally assured novel. Basically, it's one thing to write a good fifty pages, but it's another to write a good 200 pages, and on most occasions most agents need to see that you're able to do that. The beginning of your book is the place where all of this is set in motion. Not convinced? As an exercise, re-watch a film with a powerful closing sequence. Question why you find the story emotional, and also the way it manages to prick those emotions. The building blocks to your answers will always be steeped in what's revealed at the film's beginning.

The second reason to have finished the full manuscript is because – as discussed earlier – what if an agent gets in touch and asks to read more? On the one hand, it's great that your writing has done enough to warrant their attention, but on the other, it's such an unnecessary risk of the momentum you've gained to have to awkwardly ask whether they'd mind waiting a couple of months while you finish the manuscript. Yes, they'll probably be willing to wait because your work clearly shows promise, but there's no escaping the sense of disappointment they're likely to feel at not being able to continue with the story that hooked their interest. Assuming you have a long-held ambition to become a published author, why not take yourself seriously enough to work on the basis that an agent could well contact you to ask to see the full manuscript?

## Does a prologue count as a first chapter?

Prologues polarise opinion. Obviously they can be used very effectively but, in the same way that writing from the perspective of more than one character has the potential to confuse readers, a prologue runs the risk of losing people because it essentially requires someone to start your book *twice*. This is why they can be such a thorny issue with agents, and why many need convincing that a prologue is absolutely essential to a story. In assessing your own prologue, it may be worth considering the following:

- is it a short, memorable opening that whets the appetite for the proper opening of the book, and also works as a self-contained scene separate to the main narrative?

- does it steer clear of exposition, and/or could the scene-setting and character dynamics included be woven into your main narrative?

- is it intriguing? Does it make the reader want to get stuck into Chapter One of your book, or does it instead act as a distraction that puts distance between the reader and the beginning of your story?

- what are you trying to do in your prologue that can't be achieved within the narrative of the rest of your book?

- are the contents of your prologue *really* worth making your reader start the book twice?

In terms of the prologue being included in the documents you include within your submission package – unless specifically stated otherwise somewhere in the agency guidelines – as long as it's not incredibly long, then it's probably alright to submit alongside the opening three chapters. If the quality of the writing is good, you've approached the right agent in a professional manner, and you have an intriguing hook, they should want to read your manuscript regardless. The inclusion of a two- or three-page prologue won't be the reason for your book being turned down.

## How important is the opening line of my book?

There's a mythology around the opening line of a book, but acclaimed opening lines are only ever lauded if the book that follows is any good. In reality it's no more important than the title, the way your first chapter ends, the way Chapter Two begins, and so on. It's just one element of the overall package that is 'Your Book'.

If you do have a brilliant opening sentence, though, that's great. In an ideal world, the first words of your book should set up what's to come for the reader, and lead into an intriguing opening section that compels them to continue. But if you can't achieve that within your opening line, don't panic: provided the rest of your opening – and the rest of the book, for that matter – gives the reader a reason to continue reading, you're on to a winner.

## Do the opening chapters need to contain anything in particular?

This isn't an easy thing to summarise because every book has its specific needs. To start with, why not think like a reader? What would *you* want from the opening of a book in the mould of what you've written? Does yours do that? In general, a good beginning to a story needs to contain writing that introduces the tone, themes, main characters and writing style that carry through the book as a whole. You want to words in your opening section are the first snowflakes that will ultimately cause the avalanche. Here are some things to consider that might help achieve this:

**Setting.** Most novels will have more than one setting because of the way the plot evolves. To take an obvious example, a classic scenario for writers in the fantasy genre is for readers to meet their protagonist in their 'real-world' setting before finding their way into the imaginary realm in which the majority of the novel is set. The creation of this second world should arguably be where their work is judged, so things need to move at a good pace if it's to appear in the chapters submitted to an agent. General questions to ask that apply across all types of writing are: Have you spent too much time setting up the story? Will a reader be patient enough to allow you to do that?

**Voice.** How are you telling the story? The concept of 'voice' is an elusive one but – alongside good writing and an intriguing concept – definitely something agents and editors are looking for in a submission. The main reason for a unique narrative 'voice' being a difficult concept to grasp is that it's somehow welded into all of the decisions that have gone into the words a writer has and hasn't selected to use. How have they phrased things, and from which angle? Why have they said it *that* way? It's just something that's either there or isn't, but agents immediately recognise when it is because it's intrinsic to writing that strikes a chord and has an identity. Glance at a passage from *Catcher in the Rye* or read some Cormac McCarthy, for example. Somehow you know exactly who that writing belongs to.

**Protagonist(s).** It's essential to introduce your protagonist in the opening of your book, and ensure that your reader invests in them. If you're a writer with a dual or multi- perspective narrative, be careful before moving your reader to the viewpoint of another character straightaway. The opening chapters are a place for a reader to bond with their protagonist, and asking them to move into the mindset of another character runs the risk of basically asking them to start again. Yes, of course you'll be able to reel off examples of writing from multiple points of view that has worked to stunning effect, but just be aware that breaking the rhythm and understanding you've established with your reader through one character is a high-wire act.

**Your opening scene(s).** Are you starting at the right moment of your story to grip your reader? Maybe you've decided to start the book with a crucial scene towards the middle (or end) of your protagonist's journey in order to make your reader think 'How the hell did they end up in that situation?' Only by having written the full novel can you make a decision regarding your opening scene with any degree of certainty. Whatever you decide, though, come the end of your opening chapters an agent (but also anyone you want to read and become invested in your book) needs to understand the sort of book you're writing, who it's about and what's at stake. An immediacy in your opening scenes can help you achieve this to great effect.

# How should I format my manuscript?

Follow the agency guidelines of each agent you query as closely as possible. Unfortunately, these may differ slightly from one another, but try to remember this isn't something that's been contrived to trip you up; it's there to provide the agent with a more comfortable reading experience that's more conducive to them focusing on nothing other than your writing. Those that ignore these formatting requirements run the risk of agents giving their submission short shrift. It might seem trivial, but if you don't send your documents to an agent in a way an agent expects then this forms a negative first impression of your book, and you as an author. Do you come across as professional, organised and someone who wants to give your writing the chance it deserves? Or as a writer without attention to detail or the work ethic to bring the best out of the ideas they have?

On a subliminal level, agents do ask these sorts of questions as they read through your work, which is the only evidence from which they can draw their conclusions. Regardless of whether the content of your book is something that appeals to them, a failure to comply with simple formatting guidelines is a sure-fire way to get off to a bad start and also draw attention away from your writing. Here are some quick things to consider that could prevent this:

**Font type and font size.** Formatting guidelines are all about keeping your manuscript easy to read. Times New Roman or Arial should do the trick, but (again) check the submission guidelines of each agency to be sure. Crazy fonts are a no-no. It's a gimmick, and devices like this could lead to an agent questioning why your writing isn't working harder to do the talking for you. There will almost certainly be a recommended type size within the submission guideline information, but if you have worked in a different size to the one stated and forget to change it before submitting then – provided it's still easy for the agent to read – don't stress too much.

**Line spacing.** When formatting your manuscript, it's best to work with 1.5 line spacing (check agency guidelines). Not only does this keep things easy to read, but if an agent decides to read a printed version then it leaves them a bit of space to make notes. If you do have to change the line spacing of your opening chapters to adhere to the formatting guidelines of a particular agency, it might be worth running through the document again to check page-break spacing before you send it off.

**Making it look like a book.** There really is no need to try and format your manuscript so that it looks like a printed book. It's not your job to do this; in fact, it's a waste of time that may leave an agent wondering why you didn't spend as much time tightening the manuscript as you did tweaking the formatting.

**Illustrations.** Don't include them. At best, any associated artwork might be considered a pleasant extra but at worst, an interference that draws attention away from your manuscript. If you've planned to have a map at the beginning of your book then it might be useful to include this as supplementary material, but it's still unlikely to have any bearing on an agent showing an interest in representing your book. Remember, you're submitting to them *as an author* and will be judged on the strength of your writing alone. If you're submitting a children's picture book, you could include a page spread document (which could contain rough artwork purely for illustrative purposes) as a way to express the story's rhythm, but don't make the mistake of appearing prescriptive. If you're pitching to an agent as a writer, ensure your words are the focus of submission.

## Should my opening chapters be in one file?

Yes. Give the agent as little to do as possible, starting with not asking them to open three separate files to read your opening chapters. A reason for one single file being requested, for example, is that a lot of agents read on their e-reading device. They want to be able to scroll through the pages without breaking to close a window, search for, and then open another file. (To you, this might sound like not much of an issue, but imagine having to go this for fifty unsolicited submissions.)

Make it easy for the agent to keep their concentration on nothing other than your manuscript.

This being said, always check agency guidelines. Some agencies might ask for the first chapter to be pasted into the body of your initial email, for example.

## Does it matter if my opening chapters exceed the maximum word count?

In general, it's best not to take liberties bur rather to respect the maximum word count. However, if you're *just* over then don't panic too much; if an agent's enjoying your work, they're not going to stop as soon as they hit word 10,001. Writers who show a blatant disregard for the requested word count, though, are just chancing their arm. If you haven't done enough to convince an agent by the time Chapter Three comes to a close then – if they haven't done so already – they'll stop reading.

Also, although different genres and styles of writing come with slightly different expectations, agents might question the tightness of a manuscript that exceeds 10,000 words after only three chapters.

## Do agents read everything a writer sends them?

No. Every submission does get read, but only up to the point an agent feels it's not for them. This is why it's so important to do your research, be professional in your approach and make sure your opening chapters are as good and as engaging as they can be.

When writers hear the number of submissions an agent receives each week they can adopt a cynical attitude to the idea that they read everything. And to an extent they're right to do so. If your submission comprises a poorly written covering letter addressed to no one in particular, mentions a book for 5–8 year-olds when no one at the agency represents children's fiction, and is written in 16–point Comic Sans then, quite rightly, your full submission package will not get read. In fact, depending on the size of the agency, it would probably be dismissed even before it reaches an agent – an agency reader or an agent's assistant wouldn't recommend the submission being worth their time.

But where polished, intriguing submissions tailored to the tastes of individual agents are concerned, fuller attention is guaranteed. The agent it has been addressed to will then read for as long as they need to come to a decision on whether or not it's something they're interested in representing.

## What happens after an agent has read the opening of my book?

Assuming an agent has been hooked enough by your submission to read it in full, they'll get in touch to ask to read the full manuscript. They will then do so but with perhaps a closer eye on your synopsis, and some further thinking about how the book could fit in with both their list of authors and what certain commissioning editors are looking out for. (At this stage, writers who have made the mistake of not having finished the manuscript ahead of submitting to agents can get caught out.) The vast majority of agents who ask to read a manuscript in full will take the time to offer their thoughts even if they decide against offering representation. And those that remain interested in representing an author after reading a full manuscript will call or email again to arrange a meeting in person to discuss the book further and get a sense of what it might be like to work together.

Agents not interested in a submission will send either a standard rejection letter or, if they have time, a bespoke rejection letter with constructive feedback. This could include a bit of detail on the elements of your writing they did enjoy, and the reasons behind why they didn't feel it was for them at this moment in time. Even though a bespoke rejection letter ultimately amounts to a rejection in the same way a template letter does, it is actually something a writer should draw encouragement from. The agent in question has read, considered, and recognised there's something there in your work, and taken time out of their day – and away from all of the other unsolicited manuscripts piled up waiting for them – to give you their thoughts. This advice could end up proving invaluable as you begin to rework your manuscript, and could also perhaps be taken as an indicator that, with a few changes, your book is heading in the right direction.

# PART III

*Following submission*

# In between submissions

So, you've researched the agents you think are likely to be interested in representing your book and tailored your covering letter to each of them. Your email has your synopsis attached, providing a concise retelling of the major plot points within your narrative. Next you attach your opening chapters, which are as good as you can possibly make them. Then you read your covering letter through one more time, triple-checking no mistakes have crept in (if you've been submitting to a number of agents, have you got their name right? Have you looked back through their submission guidelines?). At which point, there's nothing more to be done than click 'Send'.

So now what? Is it just a case of sit and wait …?

## How long do agents take to respond to a submission?

Generally, most agencies state as part of their submission guidelines that writers who send in unsolicited manuscripts can expect to wait between six and eight weeks before they receive a reply. This allows for hectic periods (book fairs being a good example) and any holidays or other personal circumstances that might mean an agent is unable to look through as many unsolicited submissions as they usually do. Also remember agents may read all unsolicited submissions in the order in which they receive them, meaning if yours happens to be at the top of the pile they might get back to you a bit quicker.

For organisational purposes, at the point of digging out an agent's submission guidelines why not note down the wait-time for each agent? In querying several agents, it can be easy to lose track of these dates, and this will at least help keep your expectations (and anxiety levels) in check when waiting for a reply.

Some agents may have an automatic reply set up to notify writers their work has reached their submissions inbox, so don't feel the need to add a read receipt to your email.

## Are agents guaranteed to reply to an approach for representation?

Unfortunately not, but you have to work on the basis that the majority do. Agents are only human, so some submissions do slip through the net but generally (unless a covering letter/writing sample is either rude, really below the required standard or wide of the mark in terms of the reading interests of the agent) they will do their best to respond within the period of time stated on the agency website. Like anyone else in any other line of work, though, particularly busy periods (book fairs, existing clients submitting drafts of their work, personal reasons) can be responsible for delays.

If you still haven't heard back from an agent after sending a courteous chaser email, it's best to be pragmatic and write off being represented by them. Yes, in most cases you *do* need an agent for your book to be acquired by a traditional publishing house, but don't allow yourself to lose sight of the fact that it's *you* who's looking to employ them. No matter how good a fit you thought an agent might've been for your book, it's probably not worth being too despondent about someone who hasn't felt moved to respond to your approach for representation. Send one polite chaser email and then chalk it up as their loss and not yours.

## I've realised there's a mistake in my submission. What do I do?

To be honest, there's probably not a lot you can do. You have to work on the basis that your book gets one shot at grabbing an agent's attention; they have too many other writers (either those they represent or the ones alongside you in their unsolicited submissions folder) to deal with follow-up explainer emails. Send one email, make sure it's addressed to the right person, the correct files are attached and you stick to agency submission guidelines as closely as possible.

It's not necessarily all doom and gloom if you do realise a mistake has sneaked into your submission, though. It happens, and so long as your documents don't contain consistent, glaring errors then an agent is always likely to continue reading and make a call based on the overall standard of your writing and book concept. If you make a typo, for example, your work will not be dismissed – so don't get into a flap and start resending the submission in full or tracking down their agency phone number to explain because, if anything, this is likely to annoy an agent more.

Documents riddled with spelling and grammar errors, however, can't be given the same leeway as an isolated mistake. A combination of mistakes suggests a careless attitude and, understandably, an agent is likely to have reservations about working with the author as a result. Will the writer be someone who constantly turns in work with mistakes they will have to spend time ironing out? With no absolute guarantee of being able to sell every book they represent to a publisher, agents have to weigh up their time carefully – especially as an unpublished manuscript means no earnings for them or the author – so they only want to work with writers with a professional attitude. Mistakes count against you being considered, so try to eradicate them from your submission.

## I've realised I submitted my work too early. What do I do?

This is a different type of mistake and recoverable only to a certain extent.

If you've sent your work to an agent but subsequently realised there's a major flaw in your opening chapters (or another agent has made you aware of this as part of the feedback they've just sent to you) … and that same version of the manuscript has also gone out to a dozen other agents, it's a distinct possibility each and every one of them could end up thinking the same thing and reject your work. (This sort of scenario highlights the risk of submitting to huge numbers of agents in one go.)

However, if you allow a few months to pass and tighten your manuscript up accordingly then, feasibly, you could reapproach agents on that same list. Some still won't be interested, but if you use your covering letter to make it clear you're sending a rewritten version produced after taking on board editorial feedback, they may be impressed by a willingness to absorb constructive criticism and redevelop work accordingly.

SEE ALSO *What's the most efficient way of submitting my manuscript?* page 92.

## Is it alright to send an agent a chaser email?

As discussed above, it's perfectly reasonable for you to send an agent a polite chaser email if they haven't responded to you within the expected wait-time stated on their agency website.

No matter how frustrated you might be about needing to chase, it is important to remain polite. You would at work, wouldn't you? This is no different because it's a professional environment you're looking to enter, and you have no idea of the reasons behind an agent failing to respond. It could be they're swamped with submissions after a book fair and haven't got to yours yet. It could be they've genuinely missed your submission for some reason. It could be down to illness or you submitted just before they got married. Or it could be your mistake: maybe you didn't note down the date you submitted to them and you're actually chasing them ahead of time.

And, just in case you were wondering, there are some things that are worse than a passive-aggressive chaser email. Such as calling the agency demanding to speak to the agent. Tweeting the agent in a rage. Or turning up at the agency to speak to the agent face to face. It really isn't advisable to do any of these because applying this sort of pressure isn't going to make anyone think favourably towards working with you when they come to consider your work.

# Have I 'made it' once I've had a full manuscript request?

No. It's definitely a step in the right direction, but there's still plenty of time before you've 'made it'. ('Made it' is a very subjective phrase, but if this is interpreted simply as 'Will I get published?', then working with an agent still means there's no guarantee because a publisher still might not acquire your book.) A full manuscript request does mean an agent thinks your work shows promise but if they are left feeling it doesn't deliver in the way they'd hoped or that it's not quite the right book for them to work on, they'll decide against offering representation. Obviously they will be aware of this being a huge disappointment, and may well offer some constructive criticism as a means of encouragement – advice that could be of little comfort at all, or end up proving invaluable as the author begins work on another draft.

The best-case scenario, of course, is that an agent contacts you to arrange a meeting to discuss the book further. This is known as a pre-representation meeting, and a chance for you to meet in person to have an in-depth discussion about the book and basically get to know one another a bit better. An offer of representation may follow if this meeting goes well, but whether or not you accept it depends on how you feel the meeting went and if you have other interested agents to consider.

SEE ALSO *What are the next steps once I get an agent?* page 196.

# Does a full manuscript request from an agent mean I have to give them exclusivity over the manuscript?

Most agents expect you to have sent your work out to their peers and enjoy the competition this brings (it makes for better books being published). After all, as the writer you're fully entitled to explore every possible opportunity that might be available to your book. If you receive a full manuscript request, though, some agents may ask for exclusivity over a short period of time (say seven to ten days). This is purely to take the heat out of the situation and give themselves a bit of time. But although allowing one to two weeks for them to come to a decision seems reasonable in the grand scheme of things, it's not something you have to agree to if you've already prepared submissions to other agents. (Do bear in mind that this shouldn't be confused with agents asking for exclusivity at the point of your initial submission. This would be unreasonable on their part, as it would lead writers only being able to query one agent at a time, making the submission process even more protracted and time-consuming than most writers already consider it to be)

If you do receive a full manuscript request – a positive step for any writer, as catching an agent's eye is evidence of the writing being of good quality – it's important that you update every agent to whom you've submitted your book. Agents want to know if you've received interest from one of their peers and would think it perfectly reasonable for you to send a follow-up email to let them know them that an agent at Agency Y has asked to read the manuscript in full. It shows professional courtesy to keep them informed and, because they won't want to miss out on a book that one of their competitors may end up representing, your submission will move towards the top of their 'To read' pile.

## If an agent asks to read my full manuscript, should I be charged a reading fee?

No. Reputable literary agencies work on the basis that their agents charge commission on the royalties earned by those authors they represent. This rules them out receiving any monies earned from services rendered prior to a publishing agreement being signed and a publisher paying the first instalment of their author's advance on royalties. To be clear, this is inclusive of any editorial work an agent carries out in relation to the manuscript of an author they *represent*, never mind a writer approaching them in the hope of gaining representation. This stance complies with the Association of Authors' Agents (AAA) Code of Practice; ignoring this standard would prevent an agency from being listed with the AAA, and it also means they are highly unlikely to appear within the *Writers' & Artists' Yearbook* (which lists members and non-members of the AAA but does not knowingly include agencies that charge reading fees).

Do double-check whether you are, in fact, paying for a read and review service, however. Again, while not this isn't a necessary step for 'serious' writers to take, it is a perfectly valid way to get good, objective feedback on your manuscript from an industry professional. This should be marketed as an editing service, though, and not leave anyone under the illusion that it's a route to becoming represented. Check the credentials of the company or organisation offering the service, and make sure you're happy with what's going to be covered within the report you receive.

## What happens if one agent asks to read my manuscript in full but other agents still haven't come back to me?

Although a step forward you shouldn't allow yourself to get too excited. There's still the possibility the agent in question will say 'Thanks ... but no thanks'. Make no mistake, though, a full manuscript request is a good position to be in. It shows there's something in your writing and/or book concept to warrant attention. And you can use the situation to nudge other agents you're waiting to hear back from. You researched and approached them because you genuinely thought they might be a good person to represent your book, so it's a great – and legitimate – excuse to drop them a line with a follow-up email that lets them know that, although you've had interest from another agent, you'd still love to hear from them.

In terms of being transparent and emailing the agents you're yet to hear back from to let them know of there being a show of interest in your book, although there's a good chance they'll all at least know of one another, if you don't want to name the agent who's requested to read your manuscript in full then that's fine (maybe the name of the agency is sufficient). There's no reason not to, though.

One thing *not* to do, however, is use the scenario of another agent expressing an interest in your work as a means of fabricating a 'buzz' about your book and speed up getting a response from agents. It's a relatively small industry when you break it down to solely the agents working in a genre, so if you claim to Agent X that Agent Y is interested in your manuscript and it's not true, you quickly become a name not to be trusted.

Finally, a quick note on losing sight of what's a reasonable approach to take in your email to agents still to come back to you after having received a full manuscript request. Nothing is guaranteed at this stage so keep your cool. Rather than 'Can you come back to me with your thoughts or should I just assume you're not interested?' why not go with something like 'Agents X and Y have shown an interest but I'd still love to hear your thoughts on representing my book before I move any further forward with them. Would you be able to come back to me within the next couple of weeks?' Not only is this a more professional and approachable tone, it brings into focus what should always remain the focus of any decision you take throughout the process of querying agents. It's your product, so give yourself time to consider every possible option available to it.

## While I'm waiting to hear from agents, should I work on something else?

Yes, particularly because there can be no guarantee of the book currently out on submission being the one that secures you representation. It makes complete sense, therefore, to use any wait-time as a period of creative freedom. Planning a career as a writer means you need to have an idea or two for what's next, so a six- to eight-week period seems a great opportunity to explore those possibilities, whether that means diving straight into another story or doing some hard yards where research is concerned. (Although another option, of course, is to take a bit of a break!)

## I've submitted to so many agents. How do I keep track?

Rather than sending your book out to every agent working in your corner of the market, submitting to small groups of agents (on an individual basis, of course) seems a smart way to work as it gives you the chance to take stock of and apply any feedback you're given ahead of submitting to other agents. If a couple of agents write to inform you that they won't be offering representation but then take the time to give you some pointers about why your work wasn't for them, are there any commonalities in the feedback? Do they both refer to your protagonist being too passive? Whether or not you agree, it starts to become a moot point when several people have independently said as much; it's an area of your manuscript you're going to need to rethink.

In terms of keeping track generally, a spreadsheet should help you remain organised and, provided you note down every agents expected response time, should also keep your expectations in check where sending chaser emails are concerned.

SEE ALSO *What's the most efficient way of submitting my manuscript?* page 92.

# How many new writers does an agent take on each year?

It's obviously difficult to provide a definitive figure here because it depends on the agent's workload and whether the right sort of unsolicited submissions come their way or not. Generally speaking though, the number is always going to be low. Probably one. Maybe two?

Agents with an established list of authors each turning in a new book to their respective publishers (plus a couple of yet-to-be published authors with manuscripts ready to go out to editors) might decide they're at capacity with their workload and take a break from considering unsolicited submissions entirely.

An agent actively looking to grow their list of clients, however, might be more willing to take on three or four writers in the same year. It's likely they'll have more time to invest in the editorial development of manuscripts that show promise but which need work before going out to editors.

Understandably, yet-to-be published writers can see these figures as dispiriting, especially within the context of some agents receiving well in excess of fifty submissions per week. It's a reality check though, and shines a light on the fierce level of competition your book is going to face, and how reading widely, researching agents and being prepared to rewrite (time and again) a manuscript really can give it a head-start over the competition. Not as many writers as one might think are prepared to follow these sort of steps ahead of submitting their work to an agent, leaving you with the opportunity to present a set of submission documents of a noticeably higher quality.

SEE ALSO *Should I submit to a new or more established agent?* page 90.

# There are no agents left for me to approach. What do I do?

Harsh as it may sound, you should consider this a type of feedback in itself. Being in this position probably comes down to one of three reasons:

1. **you haven't done enough research into submitting your work to anyone beyond the most recognised agents at the biggest agencies.** You need to broaden your search by considering up-and-coming literary agents who are looking to develop their list. Subscribe to *The Bookseller*, look at new agencies added to the *Writers' & Artists' Yearbook*, browse Twitter and do some digging into the names of the agents that represent debut books in your genre that have sold well of late;

2. **your work is too niche, and there isn't really a place for it in the current publishing marketplace because there's no reader demand.** Frustrating as this might be, perhaps the best thing to do in this instance is to move on with another project. This is better than getting stuck in a rut, and publishing does have a tendency to be surprised by the reading public, in that a genre-busting title breaks through. If that book happens to be in the same sort of genre as the manuscript gathering dust in your bottom drawer, you'll be perfectly placed to take advantage of agents and publishers looking to quickly service that newfound (or resurgent) market demand;

3. **it might not be ready.** If your manuscript hasn't been taken on by any of the agents that you've approached, it's time to take stock. If you've had any sort of bespoke feedback from an agent, have you gone away and reworked your manuscript accordingly? If that's the case but the agent still decided against

offering to represent you, try to focus on the positives – their interest does show you're working to a good standard – and channel those into another project. If you've received nothing more than standard rejections then you do have to face up to the fact that – for whatever reason – your manuscript either isn't to the standard required, or there just isn't a place for it in the publishing marketplace. Ask yourself whether it is truly the best you can produce, or if the manuscript can be improved? Have you managed to get the concept of the book across, and is the narrative engaging enough for the audience you're writing for? Have you sought feedback from beta readers, and have there been any there been any similarities within the comments they've made? Do you know enough about other books that are selling within the genre you're writing, and is your book likely to be of interest to the buyers of those books? Why not attend a writing or publishing event to meet other writers and also, perhaps, some agents? Have you researched and written competent, tailored submissions to literary agents that are interested in work similar to your own? Not all of these questions will be pertinent to your situation, but answering those that are in an honest fashion may help shed light on why your manuscript is falling short.

Whichever of the above applies, the most important thing is to keep going. Allow yourself to be disappointed but don't allow your creativity to be stifled by frustration; part of being a writer is to be resilient. Very, very few published authors ever achieve true success, and you have to be realistic enough to know that. Those you look to as having 'made it' are more or less guaranteed to have done so only after picking themselves up off the floor at some stage.

This is the time, then, to relieve yourself of any pressure and go back to writing because you love it. Read a lot. Then, when you're ready, go back to listening to feedback and putting your work out there. The market might work against you for Book One, Two and Three, but what if the winds of change blow in favour of Book Four? All of a sudden, despite all of those previous disappointments, you're not just a writer with a manuscript that's of interest to an agent; you're a writer with a backlist ready and waiting to be developed, and that's a great position to be in.

# Dealing with rejection and starting over

Once upon a time, every published author out there hadn't yet been discovered. They were in exactly the same position as you: pitching to agents and/or publishers, re-drafting, worrying about the quality of their writing and it being rejected. So while there's no doubt that having your work turned down is frustrating and disappointing, you shouldn't allow yourself to get too low; seek solace in being part of a club that counts your literary heroes as members, and try to take what you can from the experience.

Perhaps use of the word 'rejection' – hard and charged with negativity – is at the root of any loss of confidence writers can suffer when agents pass up the opportunity to represent them. Yes, being turned down stings, but the situation as a whole should be viewed in a more balanced way, as a temporary disappointment that can be learned from, and not one terminal to your chances of ever being published. Because there will always be someone who doesn't like your writing. It's part of the process, whether you've sold thousands of books or not. And rejection will still lurk around the corner even if you go on to become represented by an agent; publishers can reject manuscripts, sales might disappoint and readers could leave one-star reviews. It's difficult, but to accept and consider editorial feedback is one way to make your writing stronger. Could there be something in the suggestions you've had, and could rewriting accordingly improve your manuscript? If you've repeatedly received standard rejection letters from, let's say ten agents, before submitting to others can you identify why? Do you have beta readers with whom you could discuss the opening chapters of your manuscript? Is it worth taking a break from your manuscript for a month and returning to read it afresh? Are those opening chapters as tight and impactful as you'd like?

If, however, you believe your work is 'submission-ready' and you're convinced it can compete with other titles selling in your part of the market right now, then all you can do is believe in what you're doing and keep writing. Continue to look for the right agent for you, but perhaps more importantly, begin work on your next project in the meantime. This isn't you 'giving up' on your current manuscript, it's about keeping moving and being stronger for it (rather than becoming hamstrung by the stalled progress of Book One). Any agent offering to represent a writer is going to be interested in all the projects you've got up your sleeve, so to have one or two significantly developed but unpublished manuscripts ready for them to look at means you're ready to hit the ground running when you get your breakthrough.

## Why do agents typically reject a manuscript?

Assuming you've written a professional covering letter tailored to an agent who represents the type of book you've written and your opening chapters come with a solid synopsis, if you're receiving standard rejections in reply then you're going to have to face up to the fact that the writing within your opening chapters isn't doing enough. For most agents, this often comes down to the following:

- **overwriting.** Try not to rely on adverbs and similes;
- **pace.** Try to arrive at a scene late then leave it early. Prioritise getting information across at the right speed for your reader; your job is to serve the story;
- **too much too soon.** You're giving readers the back-story of leading characters and getting in the way of the main story;
- **appeal.** Does your story contain themes that can be universally understood? Do you use localised dialogue? These things can alienate readers, and does an immediately narrower audience make it more difficult for an agent to sell to a publisher?

- **lack of ambition.** Can you transport people with your words, and can you effectively raise the stakes for your characters? Does your story have something about it that means it can hold its own in a congested marketplace?

- **avoid exposition.** Always show, don't tell. Use dialogue and gestures rather than lines of explanation;

- **a combination of the above.** If a manuscript is flawed for a number of reasons then it could be that you've sent your work out too soon. Is your project something you've enjoyed writing, but not yet developed enough to grab the attention of paying readers?

If your gut instinct tells you one or more of the above applies to your book, you'll need to think about how best to rework your manuscript. Also, are you allowing enough of a cooling-off period between producing a draft and sending it out to agents? No matter how well you think you know your manuscript, not touching it and then revisiting after a few weeks provides more of a reader's take on what you've produced, and flaws you hadn't seen hitherto can then stick out like a sore thumb. Spotting and amending these yourself is much better than leaving them for an industry professional to find.

## What can I expect to receive from an agent in response to a submission?

Assuming you don't suffer the misfortune of querying an agent who, for whatever reason, fails to reply to your submission, you can expect to receive one of the following types of response.

- A template rejection email: don't take offence at a boilerplate response – it's simply there to inform you that your book isn't of interest to the agent you've queried.

- A bespoke email declining the chance to represent you. This can be a disappointment from which to take heart, though, as it could include invaluable advice on how the agent believes you should work to improve your manuscript. The agent in question might even express an interest in looking at the book again after you've taken the time to re-work these sections.

- A phone call or email to find out a bit more about the manuscript.
- A bespoke email asking you to send across your full manuscript.

## Why should I feel encouraged by a bespoke rejection letter?

Because something in your writing has compelled an industry professional (and expert in the genre of book you've written) to put time aside and offer their thoughts. Given the demands on their time, agents don't send out many of these, so it is definitely worth plugging away. They've obviously seen something in your work, and feel their suggestions might help you in reworking it and fulfilling the promise it shows. If you have limited access to people who can offer you considered editorial suggestions, this could be invaluable. It's also possible for the agent in question to finish their email by encouraging you to re-submit once your next draft is ready to go. It's a step in the right direction and, when writing can be a long and lonely business, a positive to carry into the next tranche of hard work your manuscript is set to undergo.

## Everyone says my writing is great, so why can't I get an agent?

Agent representation is unlikely to happen at the click of your fingers because of the number of variables in play, but if firm interest hasn't yet materialised despite warm words from those around you then maybe you need to consider the following:

- who's actually giving you feedback on your work? If it's your mum, partner or close friend, they're unlikely to give you the unvarnished truth about your manuscript, and this is often what a book needs to reach its potential. This isn't to say the only way forward is to 'know someone' within the industry, or to shell out on a manuscript critique, but to think carefully whether the people you know are helping you push your book forward? Do you know of people that read in the genre in which you're writing, for example? Is there a writing group you're a member of or could join? Do you have online contacts (either through social media, or a blog or website you're involved with) you can trust to give their honest opinion? It *is* scary but you're more likely to have a tighter manuscript after it has been exposed to this process; and be in no doubt, it's a process that will come your way eventually if you are to go on and have your work published;

- when speaking to aspiring authors, a lot of agents use the phrase 'it's all about the writing', although the way this is interpreted is often over-simplistic. 'It's all about the writing' *does* refer to style, turn of phrase, dialogue and pace, but, crucially, it's also about the book idea itself and how appropriate it is for your intended audience. Ask yourself honestly: while your prose might be in good shape, is the concept you're writing about the real problem you're refusing to face? Could this be the reason why agents you've approached haven't shown any interest to date?

## Should I enrol on a creative writing course or pay for an editing service?

You're under no obligation to do either, and should only go down either route provided you're comfortable with absorbing the costs as there can be no guarantee of 'success' where agent representation and/or a publishing agreement is concerned. Also, are you absolutely clear about what you're paying for? Shop around, do your research and make sure that what you're committing to will truly give your writing what it needs. Do you need a copy-edit to tidy up typos or factual inconsistencies, for example? Or do you need a developmental edit, with a report on plot structure and character arcs; the sort of things your beta readers might have mentioned and you feel you need a professional opinion on before beginning to make changes?

Affordability aside, it's hard to argue against either an editing service or a reputable writing course being useful for the development of your writing. Writers who enrol on courses, for example, are paying not only for expert guidance but also for the time and space to develop their work. This, along with being pushed to read widely and the exposure to receiving feedback on a manuscript, can have a transformative effect on a manuscript. Editing services, meanwhile, are all about your book receiving objective feedback from someone working to an industry standard. Where does it work well and in which sections does it fall short? Subjecting your writing to this sort of critique could result in an entirely different view of a manuscript, and be the catalyst for changes that take it to another level.

## Should I re-submit to an agent who has rejected my work previously?

It is fine to do this *as long as*, within the bespoke feedback the agent provided, you were encouraged to do so. There's also little point in re-submitting if you haven't incorporated their suggested changes (the vision they outlined for your book is unlikely to have changed). It's not advisable to re-submit *too* soon, though. Give any rewriting a chance to breathe and prioritise this over any urge you feel to get the manuscript back to the agent as soon as possible. Why not benefit from more of a reader's-eye view of things by taking a couple of weeks off before heading back into the fray?

To clarify: if you submit a book to an agent and they turn it down, there's nothing to stop you submitting *another* piece of work to them in future (provided it falls within the bounds of what they represent). Re-submitting a manuscript that's already been flatly rejected is surely a waste of everyone's time, though.

## I have to be 'connected' to get published, right?

If you're writing fiction, be assured that this is a myth (unless you have a high enough profile …). Yes, like in any other industry, knowing someone (a published author, an agent, an editor) is, of course, an advantage. How could being privy to bits of advice or absorbing an understanding of how things work be anything other than useful? Just being around manuscripts, authors, and industry professionals will normalise a process some believe to be impenetrable, and instil a belief that getting published is possible. And yes, there's even the chance one of these contacts could go as far as to recommend your work to someone else within the industry. But beyond this stage, nepotism counts for little else. Gone are the days where one person can see a book through the doors of a publishing house and out into the hands of readers. As discussed above, a proposal has to win over many people in a variety of roles within a publisher before it gets anywhere close to being published. Who you know counts for nothing if your writing has no merit.

Being 'connected' doesn't mean living in London, either. It's true that the majority of UK publishing houses and literary agencies are based there but slowly (by virtue of cheaper office spaces and working remotely being more accepted), the 'London-centric' nature of the industry is diversifying. This being said, where you live really isn't of immediate concern to when an agent opens your submission anyway.

# I'm not 'well known'. Can I get my non-fiction project published?

Being 'well known' can affect whether your non-fiction book gets taken on or not. This is not about being 'connected' within the publishing world per se, but rather about your profile and authenticity within the field in which you're writing. This isn't to say you have to be *famous*, just that you have the credentials to be seen as a reputable voice within the area of expertise you're writing about. Authors who don't have this type of reputation to draw on may struggle for kudos among their target reading audience (who you have to assume will have a base knowledge of the subject if they're looking to buy a book about it); this is something publishers and agents consider ahead of agreeing to work with an author.

However, it could be that your book details a remarkable experience that you've had. This will be what the book is sold on and will provide you with all the credibility you need. Or, if you're writing about something that has a universal quality to it, and your experiences mean you're able to offer a different take, this is another angle upon which a book could be sold. Look at the huge success of *H is for Hawk* by Helen Macdonald as an example. There's no doubt the author's writing background will have added great strength to the initial book proposal but the clear authenticity of Macdonald's love of falconry, and how it then became something to which she turned when grieving, overrides any formal qualifications she might be expected to have had to write a book on either subject.

# Do literary agents' pitches get rejected?

Of course. It's important to recognise that gaining agent representation isn't a guarantee of your book being acquired by a publisher. Publishing is a fiercely competitive business, and publishers always have an eye on margins, bottom lines and the need to have a decent amount of confidence in seeing a return on any investment they make in an author. It's for these very reasons that agents work so hard with debut writers to make their manuscript as good as it can be (and that it's accompanied by an attention-grabbing pitch).

If you're in a situation wherein you're represented by an agent but they fail to sell your first book, this shouldn't mean they're going to stop working with you. First, you should be working on your next book at this point anyway, so they'll be invested in the possibilities this manuscript might bring. This will keep things constructive and productive, and they'll work with you to arrange a timeline for delivery of a full draft to help maintain progress. Meanwhile, where the first manuscript is concerned, it's not uncommon for this 'book that got away' to come up trumps in the end. An editor might have loved it but may have been prevented from making an offer because they failed to get the support needed within an acquisitions meeting, for example, or a wider business decision could have been made to change the focus of their list. So, although being turned down is understandably a disappointment at the time, it may lead to another opportunity belatedly opening up for the same book. For example, what if that same editor moves to a different publisher, meets up with your agent and asks about that book they liked the pitch for but couldn't get through an acquisitions meeting? A bit of luck is needed, for sure, but this is also exactly the sort of scenario that can happen to agents who are good at networking and who have their industry ear to the ground. (And also to books with a memorable pitch!)

## How much of getting published is down to luck?

Serendipity does genuinely seem to play a part but the old adage of 'You make your own luck' is absolutely true. Without an author being committed to making their manuscript as tight as possible, and then submitting to agents they have put time into researching, any assistance from Lady Luck is destined to be nothing other than redundant.

Certain circumstances could lead to your manuscript falling in front of an agent at an opportune moment. For example, is your submission the first to drop into their inbox after a clear out? Do you send it on a slow work day? Or just before they catch a long direct train to an event? Could your submission coincide with a surge in market demand for books on a particular topic?

More importantly, though, is your book ready to impress when it gets its moment in the sun? This is the only factor you can truly control so it needs to be your sole focus. Hone your manuscript, read contemporary titles that are selling well in your part of the market, research the agents you're going to send it to and then approach them in a friendly but professional tone. To do as much means that, if serendipity *is* to play a part, at least you're set to embrace any opportunity with open arms.

# Offers of representation

An agent has been in touch to ask to read your manuscript in full, and now they're keen to speak to you at greater length. Either by email or over the phone, they make contact and ask more in-depth questions about your manuscript. They may also suggest meeting up in person. Although you don't want to get ahead of yourself, from the sounds they've been making, an offer of representation could be a possibility. It's an exciting position to be in – except, suddenly, you realise you haven't got the faintest idea about the sort of questions to ask or what to expect from such a scenario. Here are some things to consider.

## What sort of things should I ask if I meet a literary agent?

Fighting nerves, worrying about what to wear, first impressions, conversation starters, remembering questions to ask, getting there on time, your future career splayed out in front of you as you make your way across town unable to think about anything beyond how it's going to go and what you're going to say ... Meeting an agent for the first time could, on the face of it, shape up a lot like a high-stakes job interview. The similarities, however, are likely to stop at the point of the agent introducing their self.

When meeting a potential client to discuss their work (you, in this case), an agent will be keen to put you at ease and basically get down to talking about subjects in which you have a common interest, and that you're passionate about: books you love, your approach to writing, their assessment of your manuscript, and thoughts around any editorial tweaks that need to be made before it can go out to publishers. They'll talk a little about their background and are likely to ask you a bit about yours, too. It shouldn't take too long before conversation is flowing easily but it is vital to get a feel for whether you have things in common *where your manuscript is concerned*. Do you agree with the changes they're suggesting? What about the area of the market they see it being targeted towards? You can learn a lot from the questions they ask, too. Have they enquired about the next book you'd like to work on, or about the publisher or imprint you see as being an ideal home for the book?

Essentially, a pre-representation meeting is more conversation than interview ... just one that's loaded by slightly odd dynamics. For the agent, you're a potential client entering into their professional domain. They want to impress you, put you at ease, and provide a snapshot of what working with them is going to be like. But in the same breath they'll also be trying to get a sense of what working with *you* might be like, too. Creatively, are you on the same page? Are you likely to show enough trust to allow them to guide your book editorially and towards a publisher they believe to be the right fit?

Yet while agents are more practised in the scenario of pre-representation meetings, writers enter into such a conversation on a relatively equal footing. You're the author of a manuscript an agent wants to work with, develop, sell to publishers, and become the point from which a writing career blooms. Yes, as a writer you need to be aware that you meeting with a prospective agent is significant in your book being published ... but the agent can't do anything unless you choose them to accompany you on that journey, so perhaps you're not the only one who's nervous when you introduce yourselves to one another.

Taking yourself seriously as a writer has served you well thus far, so don't treat this scenario any differently. Put time aside to prepare for your meeting, even if this just means going over the same things you looked at ahead of sending your original submission to the agent. (Have you read recent titles from other authors the agent represents?)

Within the meeting itself, it makes sense to arrive ready to listen to the editorial suggestions made by the agent, but do take the chance to ask questions, whether about royalty rates or the agent's vision for the book and your career beyond it. Most agents will welcome this and hopefully the notion of no question being a silly question should become apparent not long into the meeting. You're not expected to know very much at all about the way things work as a published author, so why not find out a bit more? Is there a date by which they'd like to see a next draft, say? Are there editors at particular imprints who are likely to be interested in the book? What happens when the book goes out on submission to editors? If they want to buy it, how long will it take to get published? It's an agent's job to field questions from their writers and, on the basis they appear to be interested in adding you to their client list, you may as well start asking them from the off.

One question *not* to ask, however, is: 'So are you going to represent me?' Would you feel comfortable being put on the spot in such a way? You might both be unsure and need a day to think about things so don't blurt this out and have the meeting end on an awkward note.

## What does a representation agreement look like?

A formal offer of representation is a legal agreement signed by the author and gives an agent the right to act on their behalf. These will vary in layout but remain fairly standard in the information they present. You can expect the following to be included:

- the name of the agent offering to represent you, as well as the name of their agency;

- a declaration from the agent that they will act on your behalf in relation to submitting to publishers and any negotiations that follow, and also in receipt of monies owed;

- percentage breakdowns of commission payable per rights deal signed;
- maximum turnaround time of monies owed to be transferred;
- details of any expected costs to be incurred by the author;
- a notice period for termination of the representation agreement;
- confirmation that a third-party role can't be assigned without the author's consent;
- space for both parties to add their respective signatures.

The majority of agency representation agreements are open ended rather than fixed term. This means there will be no end date or number of books to be completed with the agent before the contract expires. This is another example of the majority of agents being open to thinking about still working with an author long after their first book is published.

## What happens if an agent is interested in Book One but Book Two is going to be in a completely different genre?

It's hard for any author to get attention for a book and become a recognised name in just one part of the market, never mind two. Given that you're an unknown debut writer, then, you must appreciate that you're making things hard for yourself and your agent.

Writers shouldn't muddle the thoughts of a prospective agent during the *initial* manuscript proposal stage of their approach. Any other projects mentioned within the covering letter, for example, should be in a similar vein as the one you're pitching. And the one you're pitching should remain the focus throughout any email back and forth after the full manuscript request. But as noted above, once you meet with an agent, it's inevitable for your discussion to turn to what's next.

In an ideal world, your follow-up book would appeal to the same audience as your first. This approach helps publishers start to think about building your 'brand' as an author within a certain part of the market. They can create complementary marketing plans and publicity campaigns if they know more books of a similar ilk are on the way. These things matter to gaining visibility with an intended audience, and agents know it adds strength to their approach of publishers because not only do they get to pitch the book, they get to pitch an author with a plan. This is definitely attractive to an editor but perhaps even more so to the sales, marketing and publicity teams that are also key players in the acquisition process.

If you'd really like your next book to be something within a different genre, though, an agent is likely to think practically about overlapping readership. If Book One is crime and Book Two is historical, because both are genres popular with most of the adult book-buying public, this might not be a big enough disparity to convince an agent this is a good idea. Pen names are an option, but it's likely an agent's advice will be for you to hold back on (not ditch entirely) the historical title until you've written a crime follow-up. How receptive you are to this early career guidance could tip the balance either for or against an agent wanting to work with you.

Attempting to publish in another genre is less problematic, however, if the distance between both reading audiences is stark. Let's use an extreme example of the author of a standalone children's book wanting to go on and publish an exposé of life as a city banker. These books are worlds apart, and it's likely the author would need to approach a second agent, who would go on to approach different editors accordingly. However, if the author is hoping to establish their name as a writer for children then their children's agent and publisher would probably want assurances that the other book would not impinge on the delivery of the next manuscript the author is working on.

# Will an agent look after me if I am accused of libel, slander or plagiarism?

They'll offer guidance, and your eventual publisher should take steps to make sure anything like this doesn't happen. If there are concerns, there should be a 'legal read', which is there to take responsibility for anything contentious enough in your manuscript to land anyone in court. This isn't a free pass, though: and while the publisher needs to take responsibility for what they publish, *you* have to do as much for what you write. And obviously any threat of legal action is likely to put a real dent in the chances of your book going on to become published.

Taking a pragmatic approach, any concerns you have about this sort of thing are probably not worth going into either at the point of sending your proposal to agents or even when they make contact to ask to read the full manuscript. This is because it's probably going to require explanation, which is only really going to take place if an agent suggests a pre-representation meeting. Definitely raise these concerns at this stage, though, because you need to be completely transparent with an agent if they're to represent you to the best of their ability. They will also be able to assess the situation quickly. If you've used song lyrics, for example, then they'll make you aware of the financial implications of clearing them for use. If you're worried about accusations of plagiarism because one of your scenes is similar to another in a recently published book, they'll work through that with you. If your book paints a well-known figure in a negative light, this is something they'll want to discuss to prevent it escalating into a legal dispute.

Being candid with your agent about any type of legal concern is important, and should happen naturally within an in-depth discussion of the book. Agents need to be aware of anything even remotely controversial or contentious in the hope that it can be dealt with ahead of the book going out to publishers. Could something have a negative impact on sales, for example? It's better for this to be a known possibility and part of the conversation rather than a surprise.

## An agent has offered representation but I'm not sure we share the same vision for my book. What do I do?

Practically and emotionally, an author and agent have to be on the same team. It's in both your interests for this to be the case. So if you have a meeting with a prospective agent and are really not sure whether they 'get' your work, it's legitimately worth considering turning down their offer of representation if one comes your way.

In the section above, a meeting with an agent was likened to more of a conversation rather than a job interview. And while this remains accurate (you should have a lot of things in common), remember that central to the discussion is the small matter of your book and career as an author. Ask questions about this; find out if you're in sync with one another. Is the agent's interpretation of the book in keeping with the way you'd envisaged the story? Are their suggestions ones you can understand and agree with? Or do you get the feeling that applying the changes they've put forward could take you away from the core principles of your characters and overall narrative?

Editorial suggestions, in an ideal world, should be a discussion and not a set of ultimatums from agent to author. As such, you should never feel forced into agreeing with every change your agent suggests. However, remember these suggestions belong to a market-savvy industry expert with a vested interest in your book being acquired by a publisher. If they think your leading character is rather passive or the novel starts in the wrong place, then try to keep your hurt feelings in check and explore the possibility that they might be right. Agents may even suggest more wholesale changes to a story (such as writing from a different character's point of view, a re-ordering of the plot, or rewriting in a style that's more likely to appeal to a particular target market).

At this point, if you feel strongly opposed to what's been suggested, take some time to think about things. Are you holding back just because the changes are going to be arduous to make and you can't face the work? Or is it that the agent doesn't share the same vision for your book? In the case of the latter then it's probably wise to continue in your search for agent representation.

In picking up on your reluctance to their editorial suggestions, the agent may well have come to this conclusion too, of course. While disappointing for both parties (though particularly for the writer if other agents are yet to have shown interest), this is ultimately the best thing for both you and your book. Why put yourself in the position of working with someone whose ideas don't match yours? A clash of ideals at this stage isn't just the beginning of the book going down the wrong road before it goes out on submission to publishers, it's a potential false start to your entire career as an author. The revised version of your manuscript will go out to editors but will the version that's published bear any resemblance to the book you dreamed of when working on draft after draft late into the evenings? Imagine having written a piece of literary historical fiction only for an agent to convince you to bring a romantic plotline to the fore. You're unsure but as a result you re-work and produce a version that's acquired by an imprint known for commercial women's fiction. On the one hand, your book has been published but, on the other, it's moved a long way from the one you originally started writing. This might not bother some writers (who believe the changes they've made have led them to producing a better book), but for some this could be problematic. Could this have been avoided by listening to your gut instinct when you first met with the agent? Were you too quick to accept their offer of representation? Did you allow the idea of getting published to overtake looking out for what was best for your book? It's vital to be open-minded and show a degree of compromise if your work is to be published (because you're a writer and not a bookseller, editor or marketeer as well) but if that means putting the fundamentals of your work on the line, then have courage to walk away.

# What if more than one agent wants to represent my book?

Informally referred to within the industry as 'beauty contests', choosing between agents should come down to a mixture of creative chemistry, trust, relatability, and getting a sense of how they're going to approach your career.

Before making any decision, make sure you have been in touch with every other agent your manuscript is still out on submission with. Receiving firm interest from just one agent is a position of leverage you're able to use to chase up by email any other agents you've queried who are yet to respond. Once they know one of their peers is interested, rest assured your manuscript will become more of a priority and they'll be quick to come back to you. After that, meeting with each interested agent should be a priority. If that means keeping people on hold until the process is complete, that's fine: it's your book and your career, so speak to who you need to and take a bit of time to think through your options. And there's no need for there to be any 'cloak and dagger' aspects to this situation, either. You don't have to disclose the names of the other agents who you've met with and/or who have subsequently made you an offer of representation, but you do need to show the requisite amount of courtesy and keep all involved in the loop of a date they can expect your decision.

Before each meeting with an agent, it's worth going back over any research you did on them ahead of submitting to them in the first place. How long have they been agenting? Which publishers and authors do they work with? Are there editors at these publishers they have in mind for your book? What are their rates of commission? If you receive more than one offer, who seems the best fit for you? Which seem to be the best fit for you? And if there's no clear-cut answer to this, it probably will have to come down to gut feeling. Who do you trust to do right by your book? Which agent do you think understands your book better, you could work with better, and 'gets' what you want to do and where you plan to go with your writing?

The author–agent relationship is at once both a very personal and very professional relationship so how you 'click' is important when, chances are, they're going to see you at the best and worst times of your life as a writer.

SEE ALSO *Should I submit to multiple agents at the same time?* page 80.

## Is it a problem for an agent if I already have an agent for books in a completely different field?

There shouldn't be, although this sort of arrangement hinges on the author being completely transparent with both agents. This is essential if both agents are to be able to manage the expectations of the respective publishers they're dealing with regarding deadlines and how any responsibilities they have in relation to one book might impinge on the delivery of another.

## How do I turn down an offer of representation?

It's awkward and you might do it with a heavy heart, but agents know this is part of the game they play. All you can do is show the sort of courtesy and respect you'd hope someone else would extend to you if the shoe were on the other foot. Be polite, explain your reasons and be appreciative of any feedback or ideas you may have taken from your meeting with them.

## Once I'm represented, will I definitely be published?

Getting an agent is a significant step, and one definitely worth celebrating, but if this were a computer game all you've done is reach the next level. The closed submission policies adopted by a lot of publishers mean an awful lot of focus is given to the process of finding a literary agent but writers shouldn't lose sight of the massive amount of work still ahead of them when they reach this stage. Given the sheer number of potential obstacles in play for a writer and their manuscript after having signed a representation agreement with an agent, a published book – never mind a long and illustrious career – can never be considered a certainty until you've got a copy in your hands.

# Working with a literary agent

Now you're represented by an agent, their job is to guide and reassure you through the publishing process, to push your manuscript until it's as polished as possible, and to be both proactive and reactive.

Proactive in the sense of plotting next steps for the book but with your career as a whole in mind; to begin dropping your book into conversation with editors they've identified as potential bidders; and in making *you* their priority in order to get a better idea of opportunities you might be open to with the current title and beyond.

Reactive in the sense that they will keep an eye on the market, the general zeitgeist, and any significant movements within the publishing industry. All of this information unfolds separately to your book, but your agent doesn't see it that way. It's their job to put everything through the filter of: how does this affect my author? Does this give us an opportunity to gain some momentum before the book goes out to publishers? Perhaps a subject you're qualified to write about has become a hot news topic, or a TV series has seen a resurgence in interest in something linked to your work. Expect your agent to give you a call and float ideas about how you could write a piece or be available to be interviewed. Reactive also applies to assessing what their writers want to work on next. Would readers of a well-received debut set at the heart of contemporary London want something similar next? And if that's what the author wants to do, but fears a couple of years are going to be needed to research and write the manuscript, what happens in the interim? Maybe nothing. Or what about all of that research carried out for the debut? Readers really responded to it and there's a growing trend for quirky city guides so ... could it be applied to a non-fiction title? Would some of the author's fiction readership buy that book as a result? And could the non-fiction title bring a new audience across to the debut novel?

It would almost certainly require a deal with another publisher and for the agent in question to have form in selling popular non-fiction guides of that ilk, but this is an example of how, provided the author is on the same page, an agent could spot an opportunity and put it forward as an idea for their client to consider.

Working with an agent also means you're highly likely to see the steelier side of their personality. After all, this is a professional who's made a career out of fighting the corner of their authors financially *and* creatively. And you stand to benefit from that first hand, but purely on the proviso of your manuscript reaching the standard they deem sufficient to send out to editors. A process that could lead to you being the one responsible for bringing out their more hard-nosed side if you continually fail to hit manuscript deadlines agreed between yourselves.

## What are the next steps once I get an agent?

Becoming a represented author is a big step to getting your book published but, such is the obsession in getting over this notorious second hurdle (the first is finishing and refining a full manuscript) that a lot of writers perhaps underestimate the potential for further difficulties and hardships ahead. As you can see from the number of steps below – and the answers to the other questions in this section – a lot of hard work remains, and your agent will be quick to remind you as much even before the ink has dried on your representation agreement.

- An agent will work with the author on their manuscript for as long as they think is necessary. They won't put a manuscript out to an editor if it's not quite up to the mark.

- When the manuscript is just about ready, they'll start putting a pitch together, perhaps floating the concept of the book to editors informally if they happen to see them.

- The manuscript will then formally go out on submission to editors. This means a tailored covering letter with the full manuscript and synopsis attached.

- There's a pause. Editors will be in touch with your agent to say it's not for them, ask further questions, or that they like it and intend to enter it for discussion as a possible acquisition. Writers can do nothing at this stage (their agent will inform them of any developments) so this is often seen as a period of creative freedom to enjoy.

- If the book is rejected by every publisher it's sent to, your agent will look at the feedback they've been given and discuss this with you. They'll keep exploring options but probably suggest it's time to begin working in earnest on your new project. Internal deadlines may be agreed between yourselves to generate momentum, while they'll also be there as a creative and editorial sounding board if there are bumps in the road with the development of the manuscript.

- If the book is well received, publisher(s) will show firm interest in your manuscript by making a bid for the rights. Your agent will make you aware of what's being offered and discuss the approach they plan to take. If one publisher is desperate to secure the rights, they may make a pre-emptive bid so that no part of the manuscript becomes available to their competitors. If more than one publisher expresses interest in acquiring rights, this becomes an auction situation. Your agent will take you through each option available.

- A publishing agreement will be signed with the publisher who acquires the rights, and the publishing house's editorial processes will click into gear.

- The editor at your publisher will send over an editorial document to your agent, who will review this with you. There could be some discussion with your editor about this, but the job of the writer is to make these edits by an agreed deadline.

- Depending on the readiness of the manuscript, there could be two or three rounds of edits, followed by a copy-edit and proofread.

- Meetings will take place about the book's place in the market, and how it's going to be pitched to booksellers.

- The author and agent will see different options for the cover. You will be able to offer your opinion on these. The same applies to any conversations around a change to your original title (although this may have happened once already after discussions with your agent). In either instance it's your publisher that has the final say.

- You may be introduced to a publicist at your publisher so that marketing and publicity options can be discussed. It's likely a publication date will have been set by this stage.

- Advanced reading copies of your book might be something your publisher does, and these will be sent out to reviewers, other authors within your genre and anyone else of influence.

- Some publishers provide training for debut authors to help them become a bit more confident in dealing with any marketing and publicity events they attend.

- Publication day arrives, sometimes marked by a gathering of friends, family and all those involved in working on the book.

## Is there a difference in the process between an agent submitting a fiction and a non-fiction book to publishers?

Agents representing writers of fiction (and biography) work a great deal on ensuring the manuscript has reached a publishable standard ahead of it going out to editors. This can mean a lot of time spent (unpaid, remember, because the book hasn't been sold yet) in email, phone, or face-to-face discussions dedicated to edits and the direction of the narrative as a whole. One obvious knock-on benefit of this is a space for a strong professional relationship to form between the agent and writer during a crucial stage of a manuscript's development. This period of time is also a formative experience for the author too, as their writing is pushed to another level by virtue of their agent's unflinching editorial demands of a manuscript they might have believed 'finished' at the point of submission.

The reason for agents pushing fiction and narrative non-fiction writers so hard ahead of sending out to editors is a simple one: books in their part of the market really have to be all about the writing. A tantalising premise for a story has the power to make someone sit up and take notice but the manuscript will quickly be discarded without elements of voice, relatable characters, stylistic flair, and a well-crafted and well-paced plot. An agent knows this, and so uses this intense period of editorial scrutiny to ensure your writing leaps off the page and convinces an editor to invest in turning it into a book.

The implication here is that non-narrative non-fiction writers aren't judged on their manuscripts in quite the same way, and that's true to an extent. A sample chapter does need to be provided (and be of a high standard) but non-narrative non-fiction projects tend to sell on the proposal alone; there is often no expectation for a manuscript to be finished before a publisher has acquired the rights.

This is because, while the manuscript obviously needs to be in great shape for the book to be published, the writing is considered an eminently more fixable problem for an editor than the other key attributes imperative to this sort of book having a chance of selling well: an author whose credentials and kudos add weight to a book with a unique take on a subject that strikes a chord with the market. Basically, without the credibility of the right author, a book (no matter how neat the concept) can be undermined from the outset, and it's this unique blend of ingredients that an agent will articulate in their proposal within the following documents:

1. covering letter (Why this book? Why Now? Why this author?);

2. chapter breakdown;

3. at least one sample chapter.

If successful, these three documents will convince an editor of: what the book is; why this is *the* author to write it (and how they can use their platform to help promote it); how the author is going to structure and relay the information contained within it; and that the author is able to write it in a manner that engages readers.

As the manuscript will (most likely) not have been completed ahead of the book proposal being sent out to publishers, their second major focus (beyond author credentials) becomes the chapter outline. An agent will therefore invest quite a good deal of time working on this with their author. Like the synopsis for a work of fiction, this outline is expected to be a roadmap of the manuscript, just more detailed. As you might imagine, it should contain the key information relayed within each section of the book, with essential headline statistics or supporting material included if necessary. Coupled with the profile of the author, it's upon this document that the fate of a non-narrative non-fiction proposal will rest. And should a publisher go on to acquire the rights, only then does the author begin writing in earnest.

SEE ALSO *Who edits my book: an agent or an editor?* page 26 and *Once a book is bought by a publisher, does an author's relationship with their agent change?* page 204.

# What if I don't agree with the editorial changes suggested by my agent?

Writers of narrative fiction and non-fiction are likely to work through several rounds of edits with an agent ahead of their manuscript going out on submission to editors. Two or three redrafts aren't uncommon, and if you're reading this as a proud owner of a yet-to-be represented manuscript that's already been through multiple drafts, that probably sounds incomprehensible right now. It's essential that you enter this process – which might not apply if your manuscript is spot on – with an open mind.

First, in deciding to see whether your book could be published, you have essentially given up total control of your story. Only the very first draft of your manuscript was for you. As soon as you ask someone to read it and see what they think, you're writing for an audience. And this is definitely the case when you formally approach a literary agent.

If the idea of making changes to your manuscript is one that fills you with dread, take heart. Every writer goes through this process, and in truth there's no need for it to be regarded as negative. Your agent has exactly the same aim as you: for your manuscript to be acquired by a publisher and to become a published book. The editorial suggestions they make aren't to inconvenience you, but rather to improve your chances of being published (and founded on an expert knowledge of books in your part of the market as well as an understanding of the sort of writing that appeals to the particular editors they plan to submit to). They also come from a position of objectivity a writer is unlikely to regain at this stage. Does such an intense, intimate relationship with your characters and story as a whole allow you to 'zoom out'? Are you the right person to view it from a general reader's point of view? This closeness and commitment to your manuscript could be the root of any errors or inconsistencies in tone that have crept in, too. Is it likely that the person who wrote Draft 1 is the same writer who wrote Draft 2? Chances are your writing will have improved, and so will your understanding and appreciation of your plot and characters.

Suggested edits made by your agent should also be viewed as a conversation rather than demands you must meet. You don't have to accept every suggested change but the fact it's been raised means there probably is an element of truth to there being a problem there somewhere. Also, even the notion of rejecting a suggested change is a useful exercise. In being able to justify its rejection, you are interrogating your manuscript and getting to the core elements of what you want it to do and how you want it to work.

If you find yourself fundamentally disagreeing with your agent about the sort of book you're writing ('This is historical fiction and while there's a relationship between two characters in a time of war, it's *not* a romance novel') then, yes, maybe there's a need to reassess whether they are the right person to represent you. The more likely scenario, however, is you *do* trust them but their suggestions are hard to take because they're asking you to see the book in a different way. This might mean more hard work ahead, but why can't (at least some of) these new ideas and fresh appreciation of your work be good for your book? Could they make your characters more well rounded, your plot tighter and more dramatic? Until now, had you just ignored that feeling about a scene being flawed? At this stage it's vital for your agent to be clinical in their feedback because it's much better to find solutions to these issues now than to have them pointed out by readers or reviewers when it's too late. This entire editorial phase is ultimately for your benefit (as a writer, you're likely to learn an awful lot from the process), and is designed not to tear things down but to do the re-building required that will leave editors in no doubt of its quality.

## Is an agent's submission to a publisher much different to the one authors send to agents?

Although intensive editorial work can be done on a narrative fiction or non-fiction project, when it comes to sending the book out on submission, the actual documents agents provide to editors are more or less exactly the same as those that unrepresented writers send to them: a tailored covering letter introducing the project (pitch, target audience, a bit about the author); the synopsis; and the full manuscript. There are subtle differences, though, such as the agent already knowing the editor (and so may have had the opportunity to mention the manuscript in conversation ahead of sending the proposal by email), the full manuscript is sent rather than just the opening chapters, and the covering letter is likely to finish by stipulating the rights available for the manuscript they're offering.

A book proposal for a non-narrative non-fiction project could also be more or less the same as what the writer submitted to the agent initially. However, given that – as noted above – it's unlikely for the book to have been written at the point of proposal, it's a vitally important document and could change drastically as a result. Like a narrative-based manuscript, the language will be looked at, but also the entire format, structure, and even the intended focus of the proposal may shift following discussions between author and agent. Could approaching the subject matter from a different angle make for a more attractive proposal, for example?

To give an idea of the contents of a non-fiction proposal, here is a list of key areas a publisher would expect to be covered, and therefore certainly something unrepresented authors can abide by in preparing to send their proposal to an agent:

- a single-page overview;
  - headline information: book title, pitch, author name, agent and agency name, contact details
  - further detail: why does this book matter now? Who is it for? The estimated length and proposed delivery date

- about the author: why they're qualified to write this book, any writing experience, information about their platform;
- chapter summaries: the key learning points of each section;
- a look at the market: the general appeal of the book and how it compares to other titles in the field;
- any potential marketing and publicity angles to consider.

## Once a book is bought by a publisher, does an author's relationship with their agent change?

In theory, once contracts are signed and you've been introduced to everyone at your publisher, this should be the point at which your agent takes a slight step back. It's accepted that a writer and editor having a positive relationship can only be of benefit in a creative sense, so an agent will move into the wings to allow this to develop.

Your agent will always be ready to step in, though. If you're not happy with editorial demands or you're unsure about what the cover your publisher has chosen says about your book, your agent is there to assess the situation and offer assistance. It's part of their job to take the sting out of a situation, negotiate a compromise, explain circumstances and, when necessary, to rattle cages to make sure everything stays on track.

While writers might end up having a stronger creative bond with their publishing house editor as that relationship grows, a general thing to remember about the nature of the author–agent relationship is that it's set up to be a longstanding one. This is indicated from the very outset, as the majority of representation agreements offered by agents are open ended. Publishers, on the other hand, generally only commit to authors for a fixed term of usually one or two books. This means a parting of the ways is always in the pipeline between a writer and the editor they're working alongside, making an agent sometimes the only constant over the course of their writing career.

Yet all of this being said, authors of non-narrative non-fiction books tend to experience the in-house editor at their publisher as their primary editorial relationship. This is simply because the manuscript is rarely complete when the author is signed, and thus it develops under the auspices of their publisher's editorial team. This could range from a straightforward edit quite similar to that of a fiction book, or – if the editor didn't entirely agree with the shape of the book at the point of acquisition – it might require a process of restructuring with the author either before or during the manuscript's compilation (such as a request to see each chapter as it's written, for example).

## How long does it take for a publisher to accept or reject a book?

A number of things can have an impact on this answer: the market demand for the book, the influence an editor holds, budgetary constraints and the general internal acquisition meeting process at a publisher. An agent could hear back from a publisher within a couple of days in a best-case scenario, or it could end up being months before they get a definitive answer (though there's likely to be a bit of dialogue between agent and editor in the case of the latter – your agent will have sent a polite chaser, and the editor will probably have given a reason for the delay).

It seems reasonable, then, to give a general estimate of a wait-time of two months. This allows for the fact that some companies don't have acquisitions meetings every week. If that's the case, the editor backing your book might have to wait for a while before they can get it on the agenda for discussion.

One thing to guarantee a speedier response from everyone the manuscript has been submitted to is for one publisher to come in with a firm offer. In this case, your agent will contact each of the other editors in question to inform them, maybe even giving them a deadline by which they have to reply.

# Why do publishers turn books down?

'Rejection' might be a word you thought you'd left behind at the point of signing with a literary agent but, unfortunately, setbacks are something you're still going to have to contend with as your career progresses, just in slightly different forms. Agents know there's still a reasonable chance that a book won't be acquired when they send it out on submission, and work hard with their authors to fine-tune book proposals or manuscript submissions in order to minimise that risk. But while the quality of a manuscript or proposal are variables in play that they have an element of control over, there are, of course, some external ones they can't do much about. Here's a list of reasons why a publisher could go on to turn a book down:

- **timing.** Shifts in market trends turn opinion against investing in the book; something too similar is being worked on by a new or existing author; an editor leaves or is tasked with changing the direction of their list;

- **subjectivity.** The book just doesn't do it for the editor;

- **money.** An editor can't offer as much for a book as an agent wants for it;

- **not enough support.** While the editor could love the book, most publishers now adopt a company-wide decision-making process, meaning if the sales team (for example) isn't convinced, a book is turned down;

- **clear-thinking.** Sometimes a publisher won't know which genre a book falls into and thus how best to reach the customer.

Having a manuscript turned down by a publisher is a disappointment your agent will feel as much as you. But while they'll encourage you to continue working on the next manuscript you're writing, they won't have ruled out the possibility of securing a deal for Book One. It's their job to have their ear to the ground in case an opportunity comes up. Publishing house editors, for example, can be good at sharing submissions in-house, which may prompt an unannounced 'Just wondering' email to land in your agent's inbox. Or a new editor or publishing imprint could come onto the scene. It's not unheard of for an agent to represent an author whose first book fails to sell but, as a result of Book Two being bought, for example, Book One ends up being acquired as part of a multi-book deal.

## What does it mean when a book 'goes to auction'?

Having your manuscript go to auction is an exciting position to be in because it means a number of publishers are interested in buying the rights and have each made bids. These bids will come in to your agent, who won't pass on precise figures to the respective parties involved, but instead indicate whether their bid has been exceeded. Obviously this situation puts you and your agent in a position of considerable strength. Specific contractual clauses have the potential to be negotiated, while the very nature of a bidding war means the advance on royalties payment will rise.

However, your agent's approach to an auction situation might not be to focus on driving up the advance. They could, of course, go for it and try and secure as large an upfront payment as possible, but, in the interests of the development of your career, they might adopt a more cautious approach given the black mark on an author's fledgling career failing to earn out an advance can have. Being the recipient of a large advance brings hype and places a lot of pressure on the book selling well. If those sales are poor after the author has received a significant amount of money, an element of culpability (perhaps unfairly) does lie with them. That being said, if a publisher is willing to invest a large amount in a book, it's because they believe in it. Investment is a clear commitment: they want to see a return on their investment so will put great effort into marketing and publicity campaigns, and this sort of exposure can increase the chances of sales going above and beyond the minimum required for a book to turn a profit.

Given the choice between two publishers, for example, an agent might actually go with a lower bid on the basis it comes from an imprint with a proven track record of successfully publishing books like their client's, and the guarantee of the book being a leading title for them (rather than one of two dozen other books put out that month by the publisher who made the larger bid).

This would mean both the writer and agent initially making less money than they could have done, but in the hope their decision to accept the lower offer is vindicated by greater exposure and better sales as a result of going with a publisher that offers a team renowned for getting things right in this part of the market. And even if this doesn't mean a life-changing amount of royalties earned from sales, the value of establishing an author's career in this way could end up being the most important thing.

SEE ALSO *What's an author advance?* page 213.

## Can a publisher make a bid for my book ahead of others?

This is certainly possible and is referred to as a 'pre-empt' (a pre-emptive offer). If a publisher tables this sort of an offer, then the implication tends to be that it's the biggest they're going to make, and only available for a certain amount of time. Their reason for doing this? To prevent other publishers from making bids and an auction situation emerging.

A pre-empt is quite a bold move from a publisher, and definitely one that should flatter a writer. But this isn't to say it should be accepted. Your agent will make you aware of what's on the table and discuss the pros and cons of what could unfold. Is this particular publisher ideal for your book, in that it would be a title they'd prioritise? Looking at the current market, could a higher advance be secured? Are they asking for world rights, and do you want to give those up when there's a chance to secure more money overall by doing smaller deals with more than one publisher? It's for situations exactly like these that having an agent on your team can be a great advantage.

## I don't like a decision made by my publisher. How does an agent help?

Your agent will help make your case but there'll also be a gentle reminder that you actively sold your manuscript to a publisher, making the book their product. You should keep your fears in check around the idea of 'The Big Bad Publisher', though. Working on the basis of your having established a good creative understanding with your agent, they should have targeted publishing house editors sensitive to what you're trying to do with your book. It's entirely likely that the editor you go on to work with is creatively in tune with you and also a reasonable person who looks for positive relationships with their authors (rather than conflict), meaning any decision you're unhappy with can become a conversation instead of an argument.

However, although your opinion will matter to the editor, you have to accept your role as the writer and part of being published is to let go. As well as editorial, part of the package your book receives by being put out by a publisher is that it passes through design, production, marketing and publicity teams. To have your eye trained on every decision they make is to be too close to a book that you've just handed over the rights to, and could well be detrimental to both your ongoing relationship with the publisher and also your focus on the next manuscript you need to be working on. And if you're absolutely adamant about pursuing an objection to a decision made, chances are your efforts are going to be futile. As part of the publishing contract you have signed, there is likely to be a clause along the lines of 'the author and agent will be consulted on the [e.g. cover, changes in the manuscript, title] but the ultimate decision remains with the publisher'.

## I'm a children's author. If my book is paired with an illustrator, how does this work?

An editor will typically approach three or four illustrators about the possibility of working on the book. They will provide sample illustrations inspired by a key scene from the book and these will be sent to the author and their agent. The author and agent will submit their preferred choice, as will the editor and other people involved in working with the department.

Once an illustrator is chosen, where possible they'll be introduced to the author. The pair could go on to form a good relationship and continue to work together in the future but their creative roles are basically treated as separate entities (separate jobs, contracts and agents) in the overall publishing process.

## What happens if my book is published but it doesn't sell?

This is another form of rejection, and depending on your expectations, could be even more disappointing than those you may have suffered at the hands of agents when you first began looking for representation.

Unfortunately this is not uncommon and can be down to a variety of factors, but what happens next? First, your agent will stick by you. Book One might have instigated their offer of representation, but the agreement you signed was for them to represent *you*, so they'll be there to guide you throughout these next steps of your career.

If an editor loves your writing and believes in the next book you're in the process of working on then, provided they have the money to invest, they will campaign for permission to buy the rights to your next book – maybe offering a lower advance on royalties, and with plans to approach the market slightly differently. This could be the slight shift you need in order for your book to start selling more, and then for sales of your previous titles to pick up, too. If, however, you signed a single-book deal and as a result of poor sales your publisher decides against taking on your next book, you go back to the drawing board with your agent (who may well have prepared for this eventuality, with suggested next steps in place based on previous discussions you've had with them). Do you continue in the same genre and try to get a deal with another publisher? Or if there's something else you've been wanting to work on, is now the time to do so?

## If an agent moves agencies, what happens to their writers?

If an agent moves agencies, their authors usually move with them. In fact, it won't have that much of an impact on writers. The *agent*, however, does feel an agency move more keenly. If their author is only one book into a two-book deal signed with a publisher while working for their previous agency, the contract remains with that agency. Again, this doesn't matter to the writer because they'll receive their royalties all the same (someone else at the agency will take charge of raising royalties and transferring the author the monies owed) but the commission earned on those royalties remain with the agency as a result. To extend this example, this means the agent will also not receive any commission on the sales royalties from their author's second book, either. Only a new deal (with the current publisher or another) signed while working for their new employer can lead to the agent once again earning commission from representing that particular author.

If an agent decides to leave the role entirely, then the writer could exercise the right to terminate their agency agreement (serving the required notice period before approaching another agent). It's likely, though, that the agency will offer to pair them with another agent.

## Why do authors and agents part company?

All writers and agents start their professional relationship with the best of intentions but, of course, sometimes things can go sour. This can be down to the stresses and strains of editorial exchanges; authors becoming dispirited by their work not being sold; a mutual acceptance from both parties that they are not as creatively suited as they first hoped; or an author might want to develop as a writer in a different type of the market and approach a different agent for representation as a result.

It's important to remember both an agent and author sign a representation agreement with a genuine shared belief that they are entering into a long-lasting professional relationship. However, without this conviction in one another (allied to a creative understanding), the development of a writing career both stand to benefit from can never emerge. A parting of ways seems logical for both under such circumstances.

# Contracts, rights and royalties

The primary focus for writers should always be the writing. Contracts, rights and royalties are as far away as can be from the creative process writers have been immersed in for so long. Inevitably, though, they do come to the fore during two of the most giddy moments in a writer's fledgling career. First, in return for a literary agent's representation, a writer agrees to the agent charging commission on any royalties earned. And second, rights, royalty rates and more besides come intertwined with a contract offered by a publisher to buy the rights to their manuscript. In both instances, an author with no prior industry knowhow might start to worry: *Am I being ripped off?*

Yet it shouldn't take long to realise that this sort of scepticism isn't necessary. As noted in earlier sections, the rate of commission charged by UK agents is more or less standardised in order for an agency to comply with the Association of Authors' Agents code of conduct, allowing authors to focus more on how creatively in sync they are with those offering to represent them. And once a representation agreement has been signed, your agent is there to guide your manuscript and put it in front of the right editor at the right publisher. The trust you build with your agent – an industry expert with a vested interest in your book being published and your career as an author – means you can be sure they'll be there to explain terms offered by a publisher and guide you through their thinking before anything is signed.

## What's an author advance?

An 'advance' is a down-payment on future royalties earned that a publisher pays out to an author ahead of their book being published in return for securing the rights to the manuscript. Small advances tend to be divided into two payments (upon signature, then on publication day) but larger advances are usually paid out in three instalments:

1. upon signature;

2. upon delivery (or acceptance) of manuscript;

3. publication day.

An advance on future royalties earned is the first money an author sees in relation to their book. It is therefore the first time their agent charges commission (typically 15 per cent on a deal with a publisher for UK rights). While an agent will be working hard to sell translation rights to publishers in different territories, or exploring opportunities for film and TV deals, the author will not receive any more money from the UK publishing deal *until* sales royalties have exceeded the advance they have already been given. Once this happens, their agent will continue to charge a rate of 15 per cent commission on those royalties earned.

With this in mind, some of you are probably thinking 'I hope to get as large an advance as possible'. And this is a completely legitimate stance to take, though it's worth considering a couple of points that come up as a result.

As noted above, bear in mind that first and foremost, a large advance comes with a great deal of pressure, particularly for a debut author. Larger advances are the ones the publishing (and sometimes national) press base headlines on, usually because they're seen as an indicator of the next book to take readers by storm. This is a reasonably fair assessment: any publisher who pays out a large advance will pour a ton of resources into making sure they at least make their money back on the money they invested, thus increasing the chance of a big publicity campaign. This is a major positive of a big advance being offered, but it's by no means a guarantee of success. No one *truly* knows how well a book is going to do, meaning the risk of a book not selling enough copies for a publisher to recoup their advance on royalties is real. This scenario could also result in a publisher being reluctant to offer the same sort of deal to the same author for a future book.

A safer bet could therefore be to go with a publisher offering a more modest advance. Pessimists might say a smaller advance indicates the publisher showing less of a commitment, but an optimist would say the chances of a book earning out this figure and starting to generate royalty payments are increased.

But why would an agent want to go for a smaller advance? Well, not all will, but it does very much depend on the circumstances. If a publisher is only offering a one-book agreement, then (after a discussion with the author) they may decide to get what they can from the deal. How well a publisher will produce and promote a book will also be taken into consideration. If it's going to be a leading title for a publisher offering a smaller advance, then it probably boosts the chances of the book doing well. Also, earning out a smaller advance means a steady flow of royalties, perhaps over a couple of years. Who's to say this won't surpass the total amount of a larger advance on the table from a larger publisher?

Ultimately, provided a book earns out its initial advance, the total sum of money a writer makes isn't actually affected by the money a publisher offers to acquire the rights. They either get the money up front or receive it in royalties. The only real difference is the support given to the book by the publisher, who will work as hard as they can to make sure they see a healthy return on their investment.

## How does an author actually get paid?

When a publisher secures the rights to a book, the first payment made to the author is an advance on royalties – a show of faith in the writer, who must deliver the manuscript to an agreed deadline as a result. After delivery and publication of the book, an author receives no further monies from the same publisher until their book has sold enough copies to earn out the advance. Once this happens, they will begin receiving royalties on every book sold as per what was agreed in their contract. Royalty statements are usually issued by a publisher every six months (however, depending on the contract, publishers can withhold anywhere between 15–25 per cent of all royalties for a period of time – which could be up to two years – to guard against 'sales on return', whereby stock is returned to a publisher by a retailer having failed to sell the copies they 'bought').

If an author is represented by an agent, any monies owed are paid to the agency account first. It's then the job of the agent to scrutinise sales figures and make sure the sums add up. This amount – less the commission owed to the agent – is then transferred to the author's bank account. No monies pass directly between a represented author and the publisher, but those authors without an agent receive sales figures and royalty statements direct ahead of money being transferred to their account. This does get paid quickly, though, with the Association of Authors' Agents code of practice stating all monies owed to an author should be paid out from an agency account within twenty-one days of it clearing.

## How do agents get paid?

This varies from agency to agency and there's no real template. Some agents are on a full salary and get nothing more; some get bonuses depending on performance; some get a salary plus commission; some have to earn back their pay in deals before getting a bonus or commission; some work purely on commission. But while there are lots of different models, the key thing is that agents don't make money from a book until its author begins doing so, and all services rendered by the agent are essentially done for free until a contract has been signed with a publisher. This publishing agreement usually comes with an advance on royalties attached to it, and this is the first amount of money an author ever receives in relation to their book being acquired.

An advance on royalties paid to the author therefore leads to an agent being able to charge their rate of commission for the first time. In the

UK, the Association of Authors' Agents state the rate of commission charged by agents should be:

- 15 per cent for UK and Commonwealth rights;
- 20 per cent for translation, US, film, TV and audio rights.

Assuming the author delivers the manuscript and the book goes on to be published, the advance on royalties could actually be the only money either author or agent earns from a book. To earn more (and for the publisher to at least recoup the money they invested in acquiring the book), it must go on to sell enough copies to surpass the up front figure paid out. Provided this does happen, the author then begins to see royalties come in and again the agent would charge commission on these.

Agents, of course, don't necessarily remain concerned solely with negotiating one deal for a manuscript. They look to sell rights to publishers in other territories, thus expanding the advance on royalties coming in and subsequently the amount of royalties on sales received by the author. If rights to the same manuscript are sold to a US publisher, for example, then as indicated above, the agent would receive a 20 per cent cut of royalties received by the author. The same goes for foreign rights deals, or sublicensing deals for TV, film and audio rights.

SEE ALSO *How do literary agents make money from my book?* page 12.

## What percentage of sales does an author take?

An author can usually expect to earn no more than 10 per cent royalties on each sale, with their agent charging a 15 per cent commission for their services (working on the basis of a UK rights deal).

It's not uncommon to see escalating royalty clauses within a publishing agreement, which help improve the figures ever so slightly in favour of the author after their book has sold over a certain number of copies. For example, an agreement could state that an author's royalty rate will rise from 10 per cent to 12 per cent if a book sells more than 10,000 copies.

A quick note on how royalties are calculated by a publisher. Royalties may be levied on net receipts or recommended retail price (RRP). Net receipts are what the publisher receives from the retailer, less any wholesale discounts. Retail price is exactly what's printed on the back of the book, which means what the author earns on each sale doesn't change regardless of how much the retailer decides to charge (although note that retail price offers are almost never made in specialist non-fiction/reference).

If all of this makes for quite stark reading, then it should really hammer home the point of not expecting to give up the day job as a result of becoming a published author. In an excellent article written for the *Writers' & Artists' Yearbook 2019*, Scott Pack, an author, editor and publisher, drills down into the outlay of a publisher to produce a paperback (taking into account the estimated costs of production, editorial, design and distribution resource), and then offsets this figure (north of £10,000) against the number of units that need to sell if they're to break even. Furthermore, this worked example presents a typical royalty percentage for an author on each paperback sold (7.5 per cent of the RRP). Working on the basis of the book being priced at £7.99, Pack's workings (which generously round up to the author taking 60p from each sale) show how 3,000 books sold would bring in a total of £1,800 royalties for the author, from which their agent then takes 15 per cent.

## What sort of rights deals do agents look to secure?

Whatever they can get, but each book really does need to be treated on its own merits. An ideal situation for an agent tends to be to negotiate the sale of rights to a manuscript to publishers operating in different territories. The reason? Cumulatively this could bring in more money, and keep royalties flowing through to the author from each respective agreement. Also, translation rights deals signed with smaller but influential publishers might mean their author has a greater chance of building up a readership in another country. Could an author end up being a bestseller in a non-English speaking country, for example?

Larger publishers, however, can obviously pay much bigger advances on royalties in return for agreements that give them rights across multiple territories, or even globally. Your agent will make you aware of all offers that come in and take you through the pros and cons of each before making a decision.

## What clauses should I expect to see in a contract from a publisher?

If a publisher wants to acquire your book, they will ask you to sign a publishing agreement. This is a binding contract your agent will go through with you carefully. It exists to offer reassurance to both sides (the publisher and the writer), and serve as a reminder of the responsibilities both parties must meet. There will be a manuscript delivery date in there, for example, so you should keep an eye on this and assess whether it's realistic (though this is likely to have been discussed beforehand). Also, although UK deals tend to be for the full term of the copyright, check for any inclusion of dates your agreement with the publisher expires and/or how many books you're expected to produce within this period of time.

A publishing agreement should state that the copyright of the manuscript belongs to the author ... but, in return for the advance on royalties and future sales royalties, that the publisher has bought the right to print or otherwise produce copies of the work and sell. This reaffirms the basic principle of an author not being expected to part with any of their own money ahead of being published. It also mitigates the high percentage of sales claimed by the publisher: in paying out an advance on royalties and turning their resources to producing (editorial, cover design, typesetting, production, distribution) and putting the book out in the marketplace (sales, distribution, marketing and publicity), they have invested a huge amount in a manuscript before a copy is ever available to buy (and with sales never a guarantee). In short, in return for being the only one to take the risks necessary for a book to be produced and then compete in the market, is it not reasonable they end up with the lion's share of money that comes in from the product they give life to?

Other basic terms included are those you'd expect to be negotiable based on the demand for your book. Royalty rates per hardback, paperback and ebook sales will be easy to spot, but your agent will have a keen eye on things such as an agreement containing world rights. This is because there's a chance it could be more lucrative to sign deals with publishers operating in different territories. Equally, though, it could also be better to agree world rights with a big-name publisher with international reach.

Everything mentioned above, of course, will have been negotiated and checked by your agent, so as the author you should take an interest and question things you don't understand, but not worry too much overall. It's the most important job of any agent representing an author to ensure the contract they agree with a publisher is fair, completely understood and in good shape.

## What are subsidiary rights?

These are the rights deals for the content of your manuscript to be used in a different medium, such as film, TV, stage or radio. While bigger agencies might be able to employ agents that operate specifically in film and TV, smaller agencies can't afford this luxury so therefore rely on an agreement with other agencies in this field. They push work their way when appropriate, with both parties accepting a slightly reduced rate of commission as a result. The amount an author earns from the company who acquires the rights remains unaffected by any such agreement.

## What are co-agents?

Subsidiary rights deals as described in the previous question are examples of co-agenting agreements. Another reason for this being a beneficial arrangement is in relation to an agent trying to sell an author's book into a foreign territory they don't have much experience in. A UK agent, for example, might refer their client's book to an agency their company has a relationship with in the United States. This American agent's greater knowledge of their home market could mean a book has a better chance of finding the right publisher. Again, this referral system between agencies doesn't affect the money taken home in royalties by the author. The commission is split between the two agents involved (usually on a fifty–fifty basis, so assuming the rate of commission for a US deal is at the standard rate of 20 per cent, the co-agent would receive 10 per cent and the primary agent the other 10 per cent, leaving the author with 80 per cent of all royalties earned from a translation deal).

## Do I need to protect my work throughout the submission process?

Copyright infringement and/or the threat of plagiarism is not something to get hung up about. It really is not worth the reputation of an agent or anyone else working in the industry to lift an idea from an unpublished author, particularly when the date and time stamp on their email submission would be clear evidence of any wrongdoing. Quite simply, if the idea is good enough to warrant stealing, it's actually a lot easier for the agent or publisher to offer an author representation or a publishing agreement. Non-disclosure agreements are also, on the whole, unnecessary. You have to have a degree of trust in the agent you're hoping will represent your work, and asking them to sign an agreement such as this doesn't show much faith in their integrity.

## I want to terminate my representation with my agent. Is there a notice period?

Stipulations around terminating your working agreement with an agent will be stated in your representation agreement and can range from being able to enact with immediate effect, or after a short notice period (usually one month, but it could be slightly longer with some agencies). Bear in mind that this same clause could be enacted by your agent, too!

SEE ALSO *Why do authors and agents part company?* page 212.

## Can I get advice on representation agreements and other contracts?

If you'd like to seek advice on any agreements you've been offered, or would like to speak to someone about specific questions you have regarding a contract, three organisations are particularly good ports in a storm. Consulting the Association of Authors' Agents code of practice is always a useful thing to do, while the Society of Authors or the Writers' Guild of Great Britain are both reliable in being able to offer next steps.

# Keep going

From a practical point of view, this book is about providing yet-to-be represented authors with straightforward, accessible advice on how to put together a professional and well thought out manuscript submission or book proposal. To achieve this, a mirror needs to be held up to a writer's manuscript (*Is it finished? Is it as good as it can be? Is it worth getting some feedback?*), and then some key questions asked of their submission documents:

- have agency submission guidelines been checked?

- is the covering letter to an appropriate agent, and does it introduce the driving force of the book (as well as you)?

- is the synopsis a matter-of-fact walkthrough of your narrative, from beginning to end?

- and is the opening of the manuscript a piece of writing that not only pulls an agent in, but sets the rest of the book up in such a way they're left disappointed by not being able to read more?

You can't control whether your writing or the concept of your book quite matches the literary tastes of an agent, but in producing a set of documents that answer these questions, you've done all you can to put your best foot forward.

Arguably, though, the most important points to take from this book revolve around the sense of perspective by which one should view the hugely complex and influential role of the literary agent (their relationship with the author in particular), and also the fiercely competitive marketplace into which a writer chasing publication enters. Hopefully this wider understanding can be of assistance in being able to rationalise any ebbs and flows in progress made as you continue in pursuit of your manuscript being published.

Agents open every unsolicited manuscript submission *wanting* it to bring them a talented new client, but also in the knowledge it's only worth their while making an offer of representation to those with an idea or style of writing they truly fall in love with. Why? Because the author–agent relationship is flawed from the beginning unless it's founded on a mutual creative understanding. It's about finding an ally; someone who'll push you creatively, champion your manuscript to editors with the right vision for your book, and being able to trust someone to broker the best possible deal for the books you write. An agent declining your request for representation, therefore, is purely saying they don't believe they can get behind your book in the all-consuming way that's required.

Being highly selective over the authors they represent is also an act of self-preservation on the part of the agent. Every client they take on generates editorial and contractual work (among other responsibilities); services they are duty-bound to provide, yet for no financial return until they successfully negotiate the sale of rights to a publisher. That agents receive money from representing a client only by charging a rate of commission on the royalties earned on such a deal surely torpedoes any lingering myth of their role being anything other than entirely aligned to the best interests of the author. It's a partnership based upon the shared goal of your book being published.

And finally, an important point to reiterate one last time: gaining agent representation is a big moment that aspiring writers of popular fiction and non-fiction can become fixated with, yet, while it's a necessary step to take if you're to be published in the traditional way, there's still a long way to go before a manuscript becomes a book. That means that if the process of gaining representation becomes a long one, do your utmost to prevent it from impinging on your writing time. Don't stagnate or become permanently disappointed by the stalled progress of one book; be optimistic about what's next. Keep reading within your genre, keep being open to feedback, keep an eye on who's selling what, keep writing and rewriting, keep practising your pitch and keep submitting your manuscript (but only to agents you think stand to be as passionate about your book as you). Writing talent and ideas all matter but working to these principles will help set you apart from the rest and are the cornerstones of how to hook an agent.

# Glossary

**acquisitions meeting**
Held within some publishing houses, and whereby a committee of people from different departments (editorial, sales, marketing and publicity) discuss books put forward by commissioning editors and decide whether a bid should be tabled.

**advance**
An 'advance' is an advance on future royalties; a down-payment a publisher pays out to an author ahead of their book being published. This is usually paid in three instalments: upon signature; upon manuscript delivery; and upon publication in return for securing the rights to their manuscript. The literary agent representing the author earns commission on the advance. The author does not receive any further monies from their publisher until enough copies of their book have been sold to 'earn out' the advance. Once money from book sales exceeds the advance paid out by the publisher, the author will begin to earn further royalties, with their agent earning commission again accordingly.

**agent**
See *literary agent*.

**auction**
Generated by multiple publishers all wanting to acquire the rights to a manuscript and tabling bids accordingly; a flattering situation for an author, and one that puts them and their agent in a position of strength in terms of negotiating particular contractual clauses. The competition between bidding publishers could drive up the advance on royalties the author is offered.

**author**
That's you! A person who has written a book, article, or other piece of original writing.

**beta reader**
Someone who reads an early draft of an author's manuscript and offers their thoughts.

**blurb**
The short piece of writing that usually appears on the back or inside cover of a book. It provides prospective readers with the essence of a book, usually by introducing the leading character(s) and central tension of a plot, or the concept upon which it is based.

**book proof**
A bound set of uncorrected reading proofs used by the sales team of a publishing house to try and generate reviews.

**commissioning editor**
An editor who can acquire titles to add to a publisher's list. They have responsibility for shaping those titles and as such, they are approached with manuscript submissions and non-fiction book proposals by agents.

## copy-editor

The copy-editor is responsible for the second stage of editing (after developmental/structural). They read a manuscript for accuracy, but particularly concentrate on highlighting grammatical errors, inconsistencies with narrative flow, writing style, clarity of message, and also check facts.

## copyright

The legal right, which the creator of an original work has, to only allow copying of the work with permission and sometimes on payment of royalties or a copyright fee. An amendment to the Copyright, Designs and Patents Act (1988) states that in the UK most works are protected for seventy years from the creator's death. The 'copyright page' at the start of a book asserts copyright ownership and author identification.

## covering letter

A letter from an author to an agent pitching their book.

## crowdfunding

A relatively new publishing model that requires a book to surpass a financial goal before it can go into production. This money comes from pledges made by readers who back the project. In return, each backer usually receives a different level of acknowledgement (based on the amount pledged) from the author within the published book.

## distributor

A company that acts as a link between publishers and retailers. The distributor can receive orders from retailers, ship books, invoice, collect revenue and deal with returns.

## editor

A person who has responsibility for the accuracy and consistency of the content of books under their auspices, and a day-to-day point of contact for authors throughout the process of a book being published.

## editorial assistant

A person who assists senior editorial staff with various administrative duties, as well as editorial tasks in preparing copy for publication.

## elevator pitch

A pithy summation of your book's central concept. You would expect to see these words appear on the front/back of your book and also on advertising. Like 'log-line', this term has made its way over from the film industry.

## illustrator

A person who designs and draws a visual rendering of a writer's source material, such as characters or settings.

## imprint

A list of books with its own brand identity owned by a publishing company.

## literary agent

Somebody whose job is to negotiate publishing contracts, involving royalties, advances and rights sales on behalf of an author, and who takes commission on their authors' royalties accordingly.

## literary scout

A person who works across multiple territories to recommend unpublished manuscripts directly to publishers, providing them with the best possible chance to secure the rights to things such as film or TV adaptations, or books in translation that have done well in overseas markets.

**manuscript**
The document you've been slaving over. This is the pre-published version of a book and the text that you submit to an agent. The rights to it are acquired by a publisher if they like what it contains.

**middle grade**
A term used within children's publishing. Lower middle-grade books are those written for 7–9 year-olds, while upper middle-grade books tend to be for 9–12 year-olds.

**page-spread**
A helicopter view of a children's picture book employed by the writer to show the pages upon which their lines of text and illustrations will appear. Page-turns play a key part in the rhythm (and humour) of a picture book, and this document helps better represent this.

**pitch**
verb and noun. The verb ('to pitch a book') is the action of describing your book to another interested party. As a noun, 'the pitch' can be used to refer to the pack of documents you put together in order to make the case for your book, or the particular set of short sentences one can use to succinctly describe what's at the heart of a book.

**nom de plume**
A pseudonym or 'pen-name' under which a writer may choose to publish their work instead of their real name.

**production department**
The department responsible for the technical aspects of planning and producing material for publication to a schedule and as specified by the client. Their work involves liaising with external editors, designers, typesetters, printers and binders.

**proofreader**
The person responsible for the last edit of a book before it goes to print. They read book proofs for errors in spelling, grammar and punctuation, but also keep an eye out for typesetting errors and to make sure page numbering is correct.

**proposal**
Used to refer to the set of documents an author (and then author and agent) make for a work of non-fiction being acquired and published by a commissioning editor.

**publicity department**
The department that works with the author and the media on 'free' publicity – e.g. reviews, features, author interviews, bookshop readings and signings, festival appearances, book tours and radio and TV interviews – when a book is published.

**publisher**
A company that acquires the rights to manuscripts, pours the necessary resources into fine-tuning and producing them, and then makes them available to the general reading public and more specialised markets. They foot the bill for the entire publishing process and keep a large percentage of money generated by sales – usually in the region of 90 per cent – as a result.

## publishing contract

An agreement between a publisher and an author by which the author grants the publisher the right to publish the work against payment of a fee, usually in the form of a royalty.

## query

'To query' an agent is the act of approaching them with an unsolicited manuscript to see if they're interested in offering representation.

## query letter

See *covering letter*.

## royalty

Money paid to a writer for the right to use his or her property, usually a percentage of sales or an agreed amount per sale.

## sales department

The department responsible for selling and marketing the publications produced by a publishing company, to bring about maximum sales and profit. Its tasks include identifying physical and digital outlets, ensuring orders and supplies of stock, and organising advertising campaigns and events.

## slush pile

A dated industry term still used informally to refer to a collection of unsolicited manuscripts. Physical 'slush piles' of manuscripts used to be a fixture of publishing house editorial departments and literary agencies, but with the majority of publishers of popular fiction and non-fiction no longer accepting unsolicited submissions and a high percentage of literary agencies now only accepting submissions by email, the physical slush pile is no more.

## structural edit

The first part of the editing process that a manuscript undergoes, with an editor interrogating the narrative structure, character arcs and the order in which information is relayed to the reader.

## submission guidelines

Instructions given by agents or publishers on how they wish to receive submissions from authors.

## subsidiary rights

Rights other than the right to publish a book in its first form, e.g. rights to adapt the book; rights to serialise it in a magazine; film and TV rights; audio, ebook, foreign and translation rights.

## synopsis

A simple single-page document for everyone working on your book to use as a point of reference. It should present how your book is revealed to the reader from beginning to end (with spoilers included).

## traditional publishing model

You write a book and a publisher goes on to acquire the rights. The book production process of design, formatting, distribution, marketing and publicity is all the responsibility of the publisher, with the author not expected to part with any money throughout.

In order to secure the rights to a book, a publisher can offer an author an advance on royalties. Upon the book selling enough copies to repay this advance on royalties, an author should receive an agreed percentage of money earned on all future sales.

**unsolicited manuscript**
A manuscript sent to someone without being requested. If a publisher states they 'don't accept unsolicited manuscripts', it means they will not look at anything they haven't asked for. This is an increasingly common stance where popular fiction and non-fiction titles are concerned. Most literary agencies, however, *do* accept unsolicited manuscripts, and encourage writers looking for representation to submit following their agency guidelines.

**YA/young adult fiction**
A term used within children's publishing to refer to books written to appeal to an audience of teenagers and above.

# Acknowledgements

A list of thank yous must begin with the huge community of writers who use writersandartists.co.uk. Your contributions genuinely help make *Writers & Artists* what it is and ensure that we continue to evolve; keep talking to us.

This book could never have been written without the dozens of UK literary agents who've appeared as speakers at W&A events across the UK. You know who you are. Particular – and unreserved – thanks go out to Juliet Pickering, Lydia Silver, Imogen Pelham, Laura Williams and Thérèse Coen for their time and expertise at the various stages of this book coming together.

I have also been incredibly fortunate to call upon Clare Povey and Jonathan Eyers for guidance. Their industry nous, good humour and ability to put a stop to my waffling mark them out as important figures in the development of this book, and as good friends.

Thanks to Alysoun Owen, whose passion for W&A knows no bounds; to Katy McAdam for being supportive of this project; and to Eden Phillips Harrington for steering the ship.

And finally to Jess, whose extraordinary understanding and generosity of spirit allowed this book to be written at the same time we learned how to become a family of three. Nothing could have channelled the mind more than to have you and Arthur to get home to. I'm a lucky man.

# Question index

*Question index*

# General Index